Lecture Notes in Computer Science 12856

More information about this subseries at http://www.springer.com/series/7409

Davinia Hernández-Leo · Reiko Hishiyama ·
Gustavo Zurita · Benjamin Weyers ·
Alexander Nolte · Hiroaki Ogata (Eds.)

Collaboration Technologies and Social Computing

27th International Conference, CollabTech 2021
Virtual Event, August 31 – September 3, 2021
Proceedings

Springer

Editors
Davinia Hernández-Leo 🔟
Department of Information
and Communication Technologies
Universitat Pompeu Fabra
Barcelona, Spain

Gustavo Zurita 🔟
Department of Management Control
and Information Systems
University of Chile
Santiago, Chile

Alexander Nolte 🔟
Institute of Computer Science
University of Tartu
Tartu, Estonia

Reiko Hishiyama 🔟
School of Creative Science
Waseda University
Tokyo, Japan

Benjamin Weyers 🔟
Human-Computer Interaction Group
University of Trier
Trier, Germany

Hiroaki Ogata 🔟
Academic Center for Computing and Media
Studies
Kyoto University
Kyoto, Japan

ISSN 0302-9743   ISSN 1611-3349 (electronic)
Lecture Notes in Computer Science
ISBN 978-3-030-85070-8   ISBN 978-3-030-85071-5 (eBook)
https://doi.org/10.1007/978-3-030-85071-5

LNCS Sublibrary: SL3 – Information Systems and Applications, incl. Internet/Web, and HCI

This Springer imprint is published by the registered company Springer Nature Switzerland AG
The registered company address is: Gewerbestrasse 11, 6330 Cham, Switzerland

Preface

This volume contains the papers presented at the 27th International Conference on Collaboration Technologies and Social Computing (CollabTech 2021). The conference was originally planned to take place in Trier, Germany. However, due to the continuing impact of the COVID-19 pandamic, CollabTech 2021 was held following an online-only format during August 31 to September 3, 2021.

CollabTech 2021 received 19 submissions, each of which was carefully reviewed by at least three Program Committee members in a double blind process. As a result, the committee decided to accept five full and four work-in-progress papers. The accepted papers present relevant, timely, and rigorous research related to theory, models, design principles, methodologies, and case studies that contribute to better understanding of the complex interaction between collaboration and technology.

This was the third year that the two major conferences, CollabTech and CRIWG, took place as one merged event focusing on innovative technical, human, and organizational approaches to expand collaboration support with an interdisciplinary perspective including computer science, management science, design science, cognitive science, and social science.

As editors, we would like to thank the authors of all CollabTech 2021 submissions and the members of the Program Committee for carefully reviewing the submissions. Our thanks also go to our sponsors who allowed us to make CollabTech 2021 attractive to participants despite the difficulties posed by the global circumstances. In addition, we attribute the success of the conference to the efforts of the Special Interest Group (SIG) on Groupware and Network Services of the Information Processing Society in Japan, the SIG on Cyberspace of the Virtual Reality Society of Japan, and the SIG on Communication Enhancement of the Human Interface Society. Last but not least, we would like to acknowledge the effort of the organizers of the conference, and thank the Steering Committee for the opportunity, trust, and guidance they provided during the whole process.

September 2021

Davinia Hernández-Leo
Reiko Hishiyama
Gustavo Zurita
Benjamin Weyers
Alexander Nolte
Hiroaki Ogata

Organization

Conference Co-chairs

Benjamin Weyers   University of Trier, Germany
Alexander Nolte   University of Tartu, Estonia
Hiroaki Ogata   University of Kyoto, Japan

Program Co-chairs

Davinia Hernández-Leo   Universitat Pompeu Fabra, Spain
Reiko Hishiyama   Waseada University, Japan
Gustavo Zurita   Universidad de Chile, Chile

Publicity Chair

Irene-Angelica Chounta   University of Tartu, Estonia

Publication Chair

Daniel Zielasko   University of Trier, Germany

Local Organizing Committee

Tilo Mentler   Trier University of Applied Science, Germany

Web Chairs

Nico Feld   University of Trier, Germany
Yuen C. Law   TEC, Costa Rica

Program Committee

Claudio Alvarez   Universidad de los Andes, Columbia
Manuela Aparicio   Universidade Nova de Lisboa, Portugal
Santi Caballe   Universitat Oberta de Catalunya, Spain
Daniela Caballero   Universidad de Chile, Chile
Heeryon Cho   Chung-Ang University, South Korea
Irene-Angelica Chounta   University of Duisburg-Essen, Germany

Hikaru Uchida	Chuo Gakuin University, Japan
Andrea Vasquez	Universidad Técnica Federico Santa María, Chile
Bahtijar Vogel	Malmö University, Sweden
Hao-Chuan Wang	University of California, USA
Mika Yasuoka	Roskilde University, Denmark
Takaya Yuizono	Japan Advanced Institute of Science and Technology, Japan
Alejandro Zunino	UNICEN, Argentina

Contents

Full Papers

Automatic Content Analysis of Student Moral Discourse in a Collaborative Learning Activity

Claudio Alvarez[1,2](✉), Gustavo Zurita[3], Andrés Carvallo[4], Pablo Ramírez[5], Eugenio Bravo[5], and Nelson Baloian[6]

[1] Facultad de Ingeniería y Ciencias Aplicadas, Universidad de los Andes, Santiago, Chile
calvarez@uandes.cl
[2] Centro de Investigación en Educación, Universidad de los Andes, Santiago, Chile
[3] Facultad de Economía y Negocios, Universidad de Chile, Santiago, Chile
gzurita@fen.uchile.cl
[4] Departamento de Ciencias de la Computación, Pontificia Universidad Católica de Chile, Santiago, Chile
[5] Escuela de Ingeniería y Ciencias, Universidad de Chile, Santiago, Chile
[6] Departamento de Ciencias de la Computación, Universidad de Chile, Santiago, Chile

Abstract. In most computer supported collaborative learning activities, the teacher monitors and/or reviews data generated by students and groups as they complete the learning tasks, in order to provide guidance and feedback. Without appropriate technological means that support the processes of collection and selection of students' generated responses, these duties can result in a high cognitive load for teachers, especially if students generate textual, qualitative content that requires real-time reviewing. In this research we deal with EthicApp, a collaborative application in which this problem is apparent, as students analyze a given ethics case individually and in small groups and deliver written judgements in each phase of the activity. We present a solution to the problem, based on enhancing EthicApp's teacher's interface with automated content analysis capabilities. This includes a dashboard that automatically displays students' most relevant contributions, and cluster visualizations that permit identifying groups of students with similar responses to activity tasks. Validation of the approach was based on a dataset comprising 4,366 comments about an academic ethics case, which were written by 520 students divided into 19 class groups. Expert judgement was applied to evaluate content analysis effectiveness at selecting comments that are both meaningful and representative of students' different views. More than 80% of comment selections were found valuable, according to experts' analysis.

Keywords: CSCL · Automated content analysis · Ethics teaching · Higher education

1 Introduction

In most collaborative learning activities, no matter if these are technology supported or not, synchronous or asynchronous, distance or face-to-face, the teacher has to monitor the

© Springer Nature Switzerland AG 2021
D. Hernández-Leo et al. (Eds.): CollabTech 2021, LNCS 12856, pp. 3–19, 2021.
https://doi.org/10.1007/978-3-030-85071-5_1

development of the activity, which includes overseeing both individual and collaborative tasks. The usual intent of these actions is to provide students guidance and feedback. Writing texts is a common task that students perform in a collaborative activity. Teachers make considerable efforts to read as many of them, so as to be able to understand students' thinking and meaning processes in the learning activity. After an activity ends, teachers will usually apply manual content analysis procedures to grade students' texts, or provide them feedback. Teachers are able to cope with these duties while the amount of text remains constrained to their available time and resources. However, if the number of students participating in the collaborative activity is large, or the instructional design of the collaborative activity is such that students generate large amounts of texts to be read and analyzed, these demands can exceed the teacher's available time and effort. Considering the possibility to scale collaborative activities to larger groups of students, the development of tools that perform automatic content analysis could have significant and beneficial implications for the teacher by allowing them to monitor and/or review the texts generated by students in real-time. In this way, the teacher can provide students with immediate guidance and feedback [1, 2], that is, by having technological tools for automatic content analysis that support the identification, selection and characterization of the most relevant responses generated by students, teachers' effort and cognitive load dealing with the work of large students cohorts can be considerably reduced, especially if students generate textual and qualitative content that needs to be reviewed in real time, or at the end of the activity [1].

In this article we propose an approach for automated content analysis in a computer-supported collaborative learning script called EthicApp [3]. With EthicApp, students are presented an ethical case and a set of related questions, to which they must respond individually and collaboratively, in three successive phases. Responses to case questions are composed of both quantitative and qualitative content. The former is based on the question including a seven-point semantic differential scale, and the latter is about the students being prompted to provide written justification for their quantitative response. The requirement of students' written justifications per each question and phase implies that large amounts of textual information are generated in the activity, and that the teacher must be capable of analyzing this information in real time, as the activity transpires. The activity concludes with a whole class discussion phase moderated with the teacher. Therefore, as the students complete their work in the preceding phases, the teacher needs to identify the most relevant comments made by the different groups of students, and understand their ethical and moral reasoning in order to discuss different views and argumentations in the final discussion phase.

In this research we set out to improve teacher's support that is provided by EthicApp by adding automated content analysis capabilities to the interface, where the content is written in Spanish. As the students submit their responses, the teacher is presented with students' most relevant comments, thus overcoming the limitations of former manual content analysis procedure, which entails difficulties with regard to time limitations of the synchronous activity, and demands considerable teacher effort. Investigations show that automated content analysis methods, with English content, similar to the presented here can be as accurate as manual content analysis [1, 4, 5].

2 Theoretical Background and Related Work

2.1 Ethics and the Relevance of Teaching It

Ethics is defined as "the study of the norms of conduct and moral judgment", and as "the reasoning of the moral meaning of human action" [6, 7]. It is a systematic approach to reason and discern between, what is good and what is bad, admirable or deplorable [8]. Ethics is an active process, known by some experts as "doing ethics"; where the people who practice it must support their beliefs and statements based on some moral reasoning. In other words, even if people believe that ethics is totally subjective, they must be able to justify their positions to others through (a) logical reasoning based on theory, context, rules, and (b) also on feelings and emotions.

Practical knowledge and skills in ethics are considered relevant in any higher education curriculum, as in the global context unethical conduct has become infamously common in different industries, as well as in the public sector. In recent years, world media has disseminated a number of cases featuring unethical corporate and individual behavior [9, 10]. This has also been the case in higher education [11, 12]. This is why the inclusion of ethics teaching has been required by accreditation institutions such as AACSB [13] (business), ABET [14] (engineering) and AAA [15] (accounting) among others; through accreditation processes that urge the higher education system to include and cover the subject of ethics, as an essential and transversal component of academic study plans [16].

Although many institutions declare that ethics education is present in their curricula, teaching ethics is not a simple endeavor [17, 18] because there are epistemological, methodological, and pedagogical differences about how students and teachers perceive ethics. In the scientific and technological domains, students are often not interested in studying philosophy and ethics, because qualitative and subjective ways of thinking seem alien to many of them. On the other hand, traditional forms of ethics education, that is, lecture-based and even case-based, have amounted to limited student participation [16, 19].

With the intention of promoting learning activities in ethics education that encourage active participation, socialization and communication of students towards the development of ethical reasoning skills, we proposed the EthicApp application [3], through which students analyze and discuss an ethical case in a process encompassing several phases, with the intent to support their moral reasoning and ethical judgment, while working collaboratively.

2.2 Moral Reasoning

Ethical reasoning is the capacity that allows a person to perceive the existence of an ethical dilemma [20]. The perception of the existence of an ethical dilemma is a precondition for the ethical conflict to be foreseeable, and consequently decisions can be made. According to [20], ethical dilemmas encompass ethical conflicts, as long as they are perceived as a problem. People often approach ethics with the initial expectation that there will be a correct answer to all the questions asked. It is important to understand that there will not always be a correct answer, but developing a personal judgment is possible [21] through realization of moral reasoning. According to [21], teaching and learning of ethics results in exercising a series of transferable skills: (a) analytical skills, as students learn to think critically and solve complex problems; (b) mental flexibility and independent thinking, considering problems from multiple perspectives, as well as the value of putting aside personal convictions to follow a discussion wherever it may lead; (c) make decisions; apply consistent principles of thought and action, and learn to determine what kind of evidence is needed to support personal opinions and choices; (d) communication skills, oral and written expressions of personal points of view, emphasizing group discussion and articulating arguments; (e) group and teamwork skills, that is, learning activities in ethics may foster a supportive environment for the development of moral reasoning within a group, where members feel safe, in a climate of mutual respect and confidentiality.

According to [22], there are stages for a person to act ethically, through their moral reasoning. First, the person must have a moral conscience to identify whether or not they face a situation associated with ethical issues [8]. In a second stage, the person will make an ethical judgment on the situation, so that, based on their moral reasoning, they will determine the various alternative measures that will be taken to deal with the situation. In the third stage, the person will choose alternative actions and deal with the situation. Finally, to face the ethical dilemma, in a fourth stage, the person decides their behavior or ethical posture, considering previous stages.

2.3 Automated Content Analysis

In recent years, automated text analysis techniques have emerged for multiple domains, such as medical literature [23], social networks [24], journalism [25] and education [2]. This has been possible following the development of language models.

In face-to-face education, automated content analysis has focused on concept extraction from student discussions [4, 26], classification [1, 5], sentiment analysis [27], interaction analysis [28] and text summarization [29].

In Massive Open Online Courses (MOOCs), uses of automated content analysis have aimed at predicting whether a student will finish the course or not. For this, students' content generated in learning tasks and assessment has been utilized, along with other information sources [30]. On the other hand, efforts have been made to explore text summarization techniques intended to facilitate reviewing students' work [31]. Given the massiveness of MOOCs, interactions of the users with each other and with the platform result in a large information yield that makes it possible to extract meaning that can be used to inform instructional design, and tailor learning activities and assessment to improve alignment with learning goals [32].

The state of the art of automatic content analysis in different application domains has been mostly developed for the English language [33]. The approach applied in this research has worked effectively with content written in Spanish [34]. On the other hand, the application presented here works in real-time; particularly the teacher has a dashboard to analyze all the discussions carried out during the activity. Another relevant aspect of the application presented in this research is the fact that content is generated in the context of a learning activity in which students respond to a set of questions throughout a sequence of phases. A major concern that arises is informing the teacher how student-generated content changes across the phases of the learning activity.

2.4 EthicApp

EthicApp is a collaborative application to support students' development of ethical discernment and moral reasoning. It is available as a web application that can be accessed by any device with a capable web browser, including desktop computers, smart phones, or tablets. EthicApp works in face-to-face or distributed settings, synchronously or asynchronously. An activity is based on an ethics case and dilemmatic questions in relation to the case. Both the ethics case and the questions are elaborated by teachers or practitioners in ethics education according to each course's requirements. The instructional design of EthicApp is depicted in Fig. 1. Reading the ethic case takes approximately 15 to 20 min, and the students are asked to do it two days before the synchronous activity takes place. During the EthicApp activity, students must answer the case questions, both individually and collaboratively in small groups of three. Each answer to a case question consists on the selection of a value in a 7-point Semantic Differential (SD) scale, which reflects the position of the student in relation to the question, together with a brief comment (text) that justifies their value selection in the SD scale.

Ethics cases in EthicApp commonly comprise three questions **Q1, Q2** and **Q3**, which are asked to the students repeatedly in three phases, see (see phases 1 to 3 in Fig. 1). The phases are as follows: (a) **phase 1 'Individual Appraisal'** – each student responds individually to the case questions, (b) **phase 2 'Appraisal Sharing'** – the students respond to the case questions with the possibility of reading, anonymously, the responses and comments of their group mates, (c) and **phase 3 'Group Discussion'** – whereas in the previous phase, the students read their group mates' responses and comments, and may discuss their points of view through a synchronous chat interface. The ways which EthicApp supports students' moral discernment and ethical reasoning consist in the process of answering the SD scales with qualitative justifications based on textual comments, which represent their discernment and individual moral reasoning. Throughout the activity phases, the students are given the chance to re-elaborate their points of view and reasoning, and in doing so consider the answers of their group mates. Lastly, the students anonymously exchange their opinions and arguments by interacting through the chat interface.

After the three phases explained above, the teacher ends the activity by moderating a **'Whole Class Discussion'** phase, in a non-anonymous and collaborative mode, with the aim that the students can understand different standpoints and opinions that emerged in the prior phases, along with case resolution alternatives that can be considered beneficial.

The functionalities that EthicApp provides the teacher are the following: (a) allows them to configure the case by reading and asking questions in the form of SD scales, prior to working with the students; (b) launch activity phases and control their transitions, which includes controlling the time available to students to submit their answers; (c) track the students who have joined the session; (d) real-time monitoring of the activity phases, through a dashboard that displays students' progress and permits access to their responses; (e) review student responses; (f) observe variations in students' responses

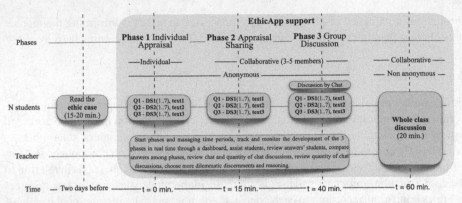

Fig. 1. EthicApp instructional design considering a 60-min classroom activity.

phase by phase; (g) review students' answers and discussions in the 'Appraisal Sharing' and 'Group Discussion' phases.

Teachers conduct the process of reviewing students' insights and reasoning through a dashboard interface, which allows real time access to students' responses, in all three phases (see Fig. 2). The dashboard displays a table comprising students' quantitative responses, and descriptive statistics of these at the group level. The dashboard indicates the most heterogeneous groups with regard to their quantitative responses, by means of a traffic light color scheme in relation to the variation coefficient of quantitative response scores in the groups. That is, a green color indicates a low variation coefficient (less than 0.5), yellow indicates a value in between 0.5 and 1.0, and red indicates a variation coefficient greater or equal than 1.0. On the other hand, the teacher can access students' qualitative content through the dashboard, which includes their comments and justifications in relation to each of the case questions. Apart from students' responses to questions, the dashboard allows the teacher to see the number of chat messages that have been exchanged by each group in the 'Group Discussion' phase. In previous research, a correlation has been observed among the heterogeneity of students' quantitative responses to case questions and the amount of chat messages exchanged through chat [3].

The evaluation of EthicApp's technical usability was carried out in [3] with 35 engineering students, obtaining a score of 79.9 on the System Usability Scale (SUS). The students highlighted the convenience of anonymity when interacting with their peers. In [35], implicit interactions were modeled and implemented in EthicApp to support group formation in appraisal sharing and group discussion phases. By these means, student grouping criteria based on bringing together students with differing views was executed implicitly and automatically by EthicApp. It was observed that by these criteria groups discussed more than with random student grouping.

2.5 Ethical Case and Dataset Under Study

The results presented in this study stem from EthicApp activities based on an ethical case developed at the Faculty of Physical and Mathematic Sciences of the University of

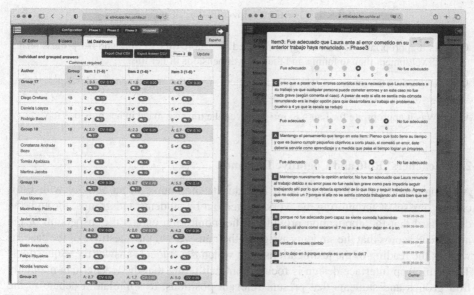

Fig. 2. Left: EthicApp's teacher dashboard, displaying results of the 'Group Discussion' phase, including students' quantitative answer scores and number of chat messages in each group. Right: Quantitative and qualitative students responses in a group. (Color figure online)

Chile (henceforth, FCFM-UCh). The ethical case, titled 'Laura', deals with an engineer of the same name, who is faced with several ethical dilemmas; the first, in relation to her work history. Laura quit her job because of technical mistakes she made, even though she knew herself competent and could have made up for the mistakes. She later found a job with a higher level of responsibility. In this context, a second ethical dilemma arose in relation to her dedication of time to family versus work, considering that she wanted to strengthen her relationship with her children and visit her aging father with health struggles, while work offered her continual attractive challenges. Finally, based on the latter, a third dilemma arose, since in her most recent job she led the development of an offer from her company to a proposal for a very ambitious project, which meant an important career advancement, but with negative environmental impact that could affect the quality of citizens and ecosystems in a certain community. In fact, her colleagues had resigned from the company because they did not agree with working on such a project. Table 1 shows the corresponding case questions.

For the present study, activity data was collected with EthicApp based on the Laura case, including a total of 520 freshmen from FCFM-UCh, organized into 19 class groups. Each class group used EthicApp only once according to the instructional design in Fig. 1. The average number of students per class group was 30 (min $= 14$, q1 $= 15$, median $= 21$, q3 $= 34$ max $= 102$). The dataset contains 4,366 student responses (i.e., justifications) to case questions, with a mean response length of 30.27 tokens (min $= 0$, q1 $= 13$, median $= 28$, q3 $= 42$, max $= 175$), excluding punctuation marks.

Table 1. Questions utilized in the 'Laura' case.

Q1	Is it appropriate for Laura to gradually dedicate more time to work and her professional development than to family and the other dimensions of her life?
Q2	Regarding the engineers who quit the project due to the impact generated, what decision seems more correct?
Q3	Was it appropriate for Laura to resign, given the mistake made in her previous job?

2.6 Teachers' Role and Cognitive Demands

A fundamental part of the teacher's role during the course of an activity with EthicApp consists of monitoring the work carried out by students and groups, through the dashboard that the application provides. The monitoring entails the inspection of the numerical scores that the students assign in their answers to the questions of the case, as well as the reading of the justifications with which the students answer these questions. The EthicApp interface design is focused on facilitating that the teacher can manually find groups and students that present relevant positions, to stimulate a debate in the 'Whole Class Discussion phase' (see Fig. 2). However, the interface does not provide the teacher with a way to easily gather and access students' most relevant responses to each case question. The teacher needs to memorize the location of such responses in the dashboard (i.e., the group in which the response originated, or the student who submitted it), and continuously scroll through the dashboard to identify groups with interesting content.

Even though the interface could be improved to provide the teacher the possibility to collect students' interesting responses and keep them easily accessible, the teacher would still need to read and make sense of students' responses in different groups as the activity transpires. The amount of content generated in the activity grows with the number of students and groups that participate (see Fig. 3). For instance, 102 students participated in the largest class group in the dataset used in this study. During phases 2 and 3 of the activity, a total of 16,175 tokens were generated in justifications. Considering a typical reading capacity of 200 to 250 words per minute, it becomes very difficult for the teacher to review this content manually, being practically unfeasible to collect the most valuable comments generated by students during the time of the synchronous activity. This process can quickly overwhelm the teacher's cognitive processing capacity, and their available time while monitoring students' synchronous activity.

The dashboard interface allows the teacher to distinguish groups that present greater differences in their responses by means of the traffic light scheme in the dashboard. If the teacher prioritizes focusing their attention only on groups and questions where the variation coefficient is greater than 0.5 (i.e., colors yellow and red), according to the analyzed dataset, it is possible to establish that the teacher must review an average of 500 tokens per question and group (see Fig. 3). With large cohorts, this task may become rather difficult. In addition, the teacher can also review the chat message exchanges in the Group Discussion phase, which adds even more cognitive effort to their role. The amount of qualitative content generated by the students in EthicApp, and the possibility that the activity is carried out by relatively large class groups, prompts for the exploration of automatic content analysis methods as a means to provide the teacher with students' most relevant content that can support their moderation of the Whole Class Discussion phase of the activity.

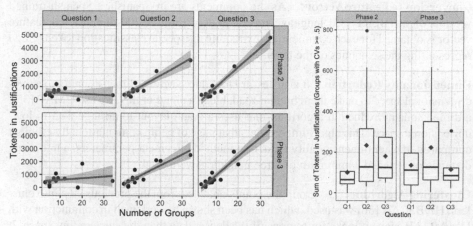

Fig. 3. Left: Total number of tokens in students' justifications per question and phase versus number of groups in the activity. Right: Distribution of number of tokens in students' justifications, per phase and question, considering heterogeneous groups. (Color figure online)

3 Methods for Automated Content Analysis

The automated content analysis methods considered in this research respond to the following goals:

1. Improve EthicApp by providing teachers a dashboard that lets them efficiently analyze students' responses in real time, within the time limitations of the synchronous activity.
2. Through automated content analysis, detect most representative and least representative students' responses, aiming to support the teacher's preparation of the 'Whole Class Discussion' phase.
3. Provide the teacher a visualization that permits easy identification groups of students with similar argumentation in their responses.

To fulfill the above goals, the automated content analysis methods explored in this research include conversion of text in students' responses to feature vectors by means of a state-of-the-art language model, dimensionality reduction, and clustering. Details on these methods are given below.

3.1 Clustering of Students' Comments

The first step is obtaining an interpretable visualization of student's comments, by converting all of these texts to feature vectors through a language model. Next, dimensionality reduction is applied to these vectors in order to reduce them to a two-dimensional space that is human-readable. Finally, clustering is applied to assign a label to shared characteristics between them. The idea is to have students with the same opinion or perspective about a question within a same cluster.

Conversion to Feature Vectors. As the comments are in Spanish, a Spanish-trained version of the BERT [33] language model is used [34]. A 700-dimensional feature vector is obtained for each comment, by extracting the special classification token (CLS) representing the semantics of the texts.

Dimensionality Reduction. It is necessary to reduce vectors' dimensionality to a two-dimensional space to make them human-readable in a plot. For this, we use UMAP [35], a dimensionality reduction algorithm that uses a graph layout to arrange data in low-dimensional space. This algorithm has the advantage of being computationally efficient compared to other dimensionality reduction methods. As meta-parameters, a minimum distance of zero and a minimum of three neighbors were used.

Clustering Algorithm: To group the points obtained from the previous step into clusters, HDBSCAN [36] was used, which has been shown to work well in conjunction with UMAP [37], since it looks for regions of the denser data than the surrounding space. It also performs well on noisy data. With regard to meta-parameters, a minimum cluster size of 10 and a leaf-based cluster selection method were used to select leaf nodes from the tree and produce many small homogeneous clusters.

Cluster Plot: Analyzing the obtained clusters and group topics for each question (Q1 to Q3), and considering phases Ph1 to Ph3, the teacher is able to compare clusters in different phases in real time.

Phase 1   **Phase 2**   **Phase 3**

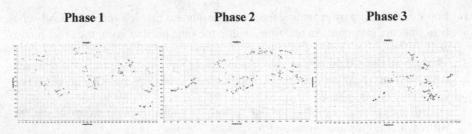

Fig. 4. Student clusters based on responses to Q1, in phases 1 to 3.

Figure 4 shows clusters of students in relation to their answers to Q1 of the 'Laura' case. In phase 1 ten clusters are observed, reflecting various possible responses to the case question. In phase 2 clusters are closer in the latent space, and the number of groups is reduced from ten to four. Fewer groups appear, with more agreement among them, after students re-elaborate their responses after reading their groupmate's responses. Next, in phase 3, the groups remain relatively close, and it can be seen that they begin to reach similar conclusions.

3.2 Most Relevant Topics in Each Cluster

In addition to obtaining the clusters and identifying groups of students who share points of view about a given question, the teacher is also presented with topics discussed in each student cluster, and a summary of the most representative and least representative comments.

3.3 Most and Least Representative Reviews

To obtain the most and least representative comments, a per-comment score is computed considering the sum of the frequencies of the words, normalized by the frequency of the most frequent word. Once these scores are obtained per sentence, scores are ordered from highest to lowest to obtain the most representative comments, and from lowest to highest to obtain the least representative ones.

Finally, to extract the most relevant topics for each cluster obtained, the same previous procedure is followed, but a score per word is computed without considering stopwords.

4 Analysis of Students' Responses

Automated content analysis was performed on the dataset described previously, containing 4,366 responses to case questions. Table 2 presents dataset summary per each question Q and phase, including the number of students' comments (i.e., responses), students' gender (M/F), and five most frequent words (T5).

As Table 2 shows, a greater number of students' qualitative responses is observed in the first phase of the activity compared to the two following phases. This is due to students' tendency to maintain their response similar to the previous phase, for which they are given the indication to respond, 'I maintain my previous response unchanged'. Regarding the most frequent words, these appear consistently throughout the phases, except for question 2, in which 'ecosystem' and 'correct' words are changed for 'staying at work' and 'decision' in the following phases. Something similar happens with question 3, where the words 'make mistakes' lose importance comparing phase 1 to the next ones. These are replaced by the word 'frustration'.

As Fig. 5 indicates, most comments in students' responses are between 20 and 40 words long. Consistently with the dataset summary, more student participation is observed in phase 1 compared to the following phases.

5 Design of EthicApp Teachers' Dashboard

Based on the automated content analysis methods considered, a dashboard interface prototype for EthicApp is proposed so that teacher can visualize student comment representation in a cluster plot, along with the most and least representative comments to each question and in each phase, in real time (see Fig. 6). Through the cluster plot, the teacher can explore comments of each student (i.e., each student's response is a point in the plot, which can be hovered over with the mouse or tapped), along with other details,

Table 2. Dataset summary. M = Male. F = Female. O = Other. T5 = Five most frequent words.

Q/Phase	Phase 1	Phase 2	Phase 3
Q1	Number of comments: 356 Gender: M 254, F 101, O 1 T5: time 231, family 199, job 197, lifestyle 145, important 95	Number of comments: 217 Gender: M 151, F 66 T5: time 124, job 123, family 108, lifestyle 82, important 47	Number of comments 273 Gender: M 194, F 78, O 1 T5: time 151, job 131, family 124, lifestyle 96, important 51
Q2	Number of comments 468 Gender: M 317, F 150, O 1 T5: project 395, give up 123, impact 107, ecosystem 76, correct 71	Number of comments 329 Gender: M 217, F 111, O 1 T5: project 270, give up 98, impact 62, stay at work 55, decision 53	Number of comments 381 Gender: M 252, F 127, O 2 T5: project 310, give up 122, impact 61, stay at work 59, decision 53
Q3	Number of comments 504 Gender: M 340, F 162, O 2 T5: error 552, job 142, give up 103, decision 83, make 60	Number of comments 356 Gender: M 234, F 121, O 1 T5: error 380, job 91, give up 81, decision 61, frustration 60	Number of comments 410 Gender: M 271, F 137, O 2 T5: error 404, job 104, give up 91, decision 76, frustration 53

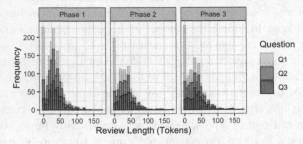

Fig. 5. Review length histograms for each phase and case question.

such as gender, value marked in the SD scale, and cluster label. In addition, from Ph2 onwards, the teacher is able to compare cluster plots corresponding to different phases.

The components of the dashboard presented in Fig. 6 are as follows: (A) Navigation Bar, which lets the teacher select questions and phases. (B) The current question being analyzed. (C) The set of most representative comments for the selected question and phase. (D) The least representative comments for the selected question and phase. (E) Cluster plot showing groups of related student comments. (F) Topics found in each cluster. (G) A bookmark manager displaying meaningful comments marked by the teacher, so that they can be easily accessible later on.

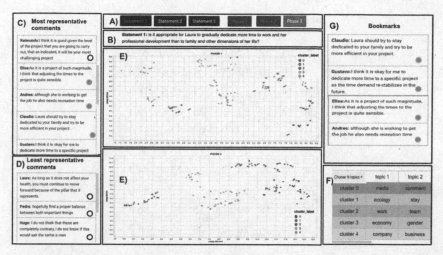

Fig. 6. Prototype of teacher's dashboard with automated content analysis.

6 Evaluation of Automated Comment Selection

6.1 Evaluation of Representative Comments

Evaluation of the automated content analysis method upon which the teacher's dashboard in Fig. 6 is based consisted in having five evaluators (i.e., a group composed of researchers and teaching assistants) code the k ($k = 10, 20, 30$) most Representative Comments (RCs) identified with the method, considering the dataset composed of 4,366 student comments. A dichotomic variable was used for coding by evaluators, with value 0 if the comment was not considered relevant by the evaluator, or 1 otherwise. Comment relevance was based on observation of well-founded arguments and consistency with the case question.

Results are shown in Table 3. The RC column showing the k number of comments per Question (Q) is followed by columns E1 to E5 denoting the sum of scores given by each evaluator to RCs. The AVG column shows the average of rows E1 to E5, that is, the average number of RCs per each question and value of k. Lastly, the AVG-% column is the percentage that results from dividing the average value by k.

The results in Table 3 show that for $k = 10$ and considering all case questions, 9 is the mode of the sum of evaluator scores, which amounts to 60% of cases. Only in case question 1, a sum of 5 is observed, and in question 3, a sum of 7. Otherwise, all evaluators considered 8 to 10 of the comments to be relevant.

Considering $k = 20$, expectedly greater variability in score sums is observed than with $k = 10$. In only two cases, sums of scores lower than 15 are observed, i.e., scores of 13 and 9 in question 1. Considering all other evaluations with $k = 20$, at least 75% of comments were considered relevant by the evaluators. In 7 out of 15 cases (47%), 90% or more were considered relevant (i.e., sum of scores 18 to 20).

Table 3. Results of the evaluation process.

	k	E1	E2	E3	E4	E5	AVG	AVG-%
Q1	10	9	10	10	5	9	8.6	86.0
	20	13	20	19	9	17	15.6	78.0
	30	23	29	27	15	25	23.8	79.3
Q2	10	8	9	9	9	9	8.8	88.0
	20	15	19	18	15	17	16.8	84.0
	30	23	29	28	22	25	25.4	84.7
Q3	10	9	9	9	8	7	8.4	84.0
	20	16	18	19	18	15	17.2	86.0
	30	24	26	29	25	23	25.4	84.7

Lastly, with $k = 30$, 60% of evaluations are 25/30 points and greater. Exceptionally, one evaluation falls under 20 points in question 1. In average, evaluations of questions 2 and 3 are similar, at 25.4 points, while evaluation of question 1 drops to an average of 23.8 points.

6.2   Estimation of Teachers' Workload

Teacher's effort reading and analyzing representative comments selected by the proposed method is estimated considering an average reading speed of 200 words per minute (WPM), and the length of each comment. However, this estimate is increased by a factor of four, as for the teacher it is necessary to read the comment, understand its meaning and relate it to the case, compare it to other comments and relate it to the actual question.

Table 4. Effort dedicated by a teacher to read selected comments (in minutes).

Q/k	10	20	30
Q1	4.6	8.9	13.8
Q2	4.3	9.1	14.1
Q3	4.2	8.9	13.9

According to figures in Table 4, we can see it takes a maximum of 4.6 min to review the top 10 most representative comments. On the other hand, to review 20, it would take 9.1 min in the worst case, and to review 30, it takes a maximum of 14.1 min. If these times are compared with what it would take for a teacher to review a total of 16,175 tokens (i.e., 81 min at 200 WPM, without considering any correction), considering comments in the largest class group of the dataset involving 102 students, and including phases 2 and 3, it is evident that the automated selection of comments can facilitate teacher's work even when monitoring large student cohorts.

7 Conclusions and Future Work

In this research we set out to solve the problem of improving teacher's support in EthicApp, a collaborative activity in which potentially large amounts of qualitative, textual content generated by the students require to be understood and considered by the teacher for the purposes of feedback and support. To automatically sample relevant student comments from their answers and conveniently present them to the teacher in a dashboard, an automated content analysis method based on the BERT [33] language model was used, together with dimensionality reduction techniques, clustering, and visualizations based on cluster plots.

By means of manually evaluating representative comments proposed by the algorithm, we found that the approach was effective at selecting valuable comments in more than 80% of cases, meaning that the teacher can effectively monitor the learning activity, and be confident that they see representative students' comments to moderate a class discussion, instead of manually traversing the former dashboard, in which they had to spot relevant comments manually, and rely on their short-term memory to consider comments and locate them when needed. Moreover, the approach permits the teacher to notice groups of students with similar viewpoints and arguments on each case question, and even see how students' responses vary from one activity phase to the next.

Evaluation of our approach was based on a dataset size atypical of common classrooms, as it was generated by 520 students. In the future, we will conduct sensitivity analyses in order to determine the reliability and accuracy of the method when applied to settings involving different cohort sizes, including those common in traditional higher education courses (i.e., 200 students and less). In addition, the proposed dashboard prototype will be implemented in EthicApp, and performance and usability tests will be conducted in order to evaluate the ease of use and utility of the solution.

References

1. Uribe, P., Jiménez, A., Araya, R., Lämsä, J., Hämäläinen, R., Viiri, J.: Automatic content analysis of computer-supported collaborative inquiry-based learning using deep networks and attention mechanisms. In: Vittorini, P., Di Mascio, T., Tarantino, L., Temperini, M., Gennari, R., De la Prieta, F. (eds.) MIS4TEL 2020. AISC, vol. 1241, pp. 95–105. Springer, Cham (2020). https://doi.org/10.1007/978-3-030-52538-5_11
2. Chang, Y.-H., Chang, C.-Y., Tseng, Y.-H.: Trends of science education research: an automatic content analysis. J. Sci. Educ. Technol. 19(4), 315–331 (2010)
3. Alvarez, C., Zurita, G., Baloian, N., Jerez, O., Peñafiel, S.: A CSCL script for supporting moral reasoning in the ethics classroom. In: Nakanishi, H., Egi, H., Chounta, I.-A., Takada, H., Ichimura, S., Hoppe, U. (eds.) CRIWG+CollabTech 2019. LNCS, vol. 11677, pp. 62–79. Springer, Cham (2019). https://doi.org/10.1007/978-3-030-28011-6_5
4. Daems, O., et al.: Using content analysis and domain ontologies to check learners' understanding of science concepts. J. Comput. Educ. 1(2), 113–131 (2014)
5. Lui, A.K.-F., Li, S.C., Choy, S.O.: An evaluation of automatic text categorization in online discussion analysis. In: Seventh IEEE International Conference on Advanced Learning Technologies (ICALT 2007). IEEE (2007)
6. Gandz, J., Hayes, N.: Teaching business ethics. J. Bus. Ethics 7(9), 657–669 (1988)

7. McCoy, C.S.: Management of values: the ethical difference in corporate policy and performance (1985)
8. Butts, D., Janie, B.: Nursing ethics: across the curriculum and into practice book review. Online J. Health Ethics **2**(2), 2 (2005)
9. Patel, P.: Engineers, ethics, and the VW scandal. IEEE Spectr. **25** (2015)
10. Zunger, J.: Computer science faces an ethics crisis. The Cambridge Analytica scandal proves it. Boston Globe **22** (2018)
11. EMOL. UC suspende hasta por un año a alumnos que participaron en copia masiva por WhatsApp (2016). https://www.emol.com/noticias/Nacional/2016/06/23/809292/UC-suspende-hasta-por-un-ano-a-alumnos-que-participaron-en-copia-masiva-por-WhatsApp.html. Accessed 1 Jan 2020
12. Leighton, P.: El alto costo de las conductas académicas deshonestas. El Mercurio (2018). http://www.economiaynegocios.cl/noticias/noticias.asp?id=452080. Accessed 1 Jan 2020
13. AACSB. Ethics Education in Business Schools (2004). https://www.aacsb.edu/~/media/AACSB/Publications/research-reports/ethics-education.ashx. Accessed 1 Jan 2020
14. ABET. Rationale for revising criteria 3 (2016). http://www.abet.org/accreditation/accreditation-criteria/accreditation-alerts/rationale-for-revising-criteria-3/. Accessed 1 Jan 2020
15. AAA, American Accounting Association. Committee on the Future Structure, Content, and Scope of Accounting Education (The Bedford Committee): Future accounting education: preparing for the expanding profession. Issues Account. Educ. **1**(1), 168–195 (1986)
16. Apostolou, B., Dull, R.B., Schleifer, L.L.: A framework for the pedagogy of accounting ethics. Account. Educ. **22**(1), 1–17 (2013)
17. Holsapple, M.A., et al.: Framing faculty and student discrepancies in engineering ethics education delivery. J. Eng. Educ. **101**(2), 169–186 (2012)
18. Felton, E.L., Sims, R.R.: Teaching business ethics: targeted outputs. J. Bus. Ethics **60**(4), 377–391 (2005)
19. Johnson, J.F., et al.: Case-based ethics education: the impact of cause complexity and outcome favorability on ethicality. J. Empirical Res. Hum. Res. Ethics **7**(3), 63–77 (2012)
20. Hunt, S.D., Vitell, S.J.: The general theory of marketing ethics: a revision and three questions. J. Macromark. **26**(2), 143–153 (2006)
21. Illingworth, S.: Approaches to Ethics in Higher Education: Teaching Ethics Across the Curriculum (2004)
22. Rafinda, A., Gál, T., Purwaningtyas, P.: Business ethics course on student moral reasoning. Oradea J. Bus. Econ. **4**(Special), 60–68 (2019)
23. Carvallo, A., et al.: Automatic document screening of medical literature using word and text embeddings in an active learning setting. Scientometrics **125**(3), 3047–3084 (2020)
24. Lai, L.S., To, W.M.: Content analysis of social media: a grounded theory approach. J. Electron. Commer. Res. **16**(2), 138 (2015)
25. Günther, E., Quandt, T.: Word counts and topic models: automated text analysis methods for digital journalism research. Digit. J. **4**(1), 75–88 (2016)
26. Chau, H., et al.: Automatic concept extraction for domain and student modeling in adaptive textbooks. Int. J. Artif. Intell. Educ. 1–27 (2020)
27. Ferreira, M., et al.: Towards automatic content analysis of social presence in transcripts of online discussions. In: Proceedings of the Tenth International Conference on Learning Analytics & Knowledge (2020)
28. Mirzaei, M., Sahebi, S., Brusilovsky, P.: Annotated examples and parameterized exercises: analyzing students' behavior patterns. In: Isotani, S., Millán, E., Ogan, A., Hastings, P., McLaren, B., Luckin, R. (eds.) AIED 2019. LNCS (LNAI), vol. 11625, pp. 308–319. Springer, Cham (2019). https://doi.org/10.1007/978-3-030-23204-7_26
29. Luo, W., et al.: Automatic summarization of student course feedback. arXiv preprint arXiv:1805.10395 (2018)

30. Zou, W., et al.: Exploring the relationship between social presence and learners' prestige in MOOC discussion forums using automated content analysis and social network analysis. Comput. Hum. Behav. **115**, 106582 (2021)
31. Moore, R.L., Oliver, K.M., Wang, C.: Setting the pace: examining cognitive processing in MOOC discussion forums with automatic text analysis. Interact. Learn. Environ. **27**(5–6), 655–669 (2019)
32. Crossley, S.A., et al.: Incorporating learning characteristics into automatic essay scoring models: what individual differences and linguistic features tell us about writing quality. J. Educ. Data Min. **8**(2), 1–19 (2016)
33. Khan, W., et al.: A survey on the state-of-the-art machine learning models in the context of NLP. Kuwait J. Sci. **43**(4) (2016)
34. Canete, J., et al.: Spanish pre-trained BERT model and evaluation data. In: PML4DC at ICLR, vol. 2020 (2020)
35. Alvarez, C., Zurita, G., Baloian, N.: Applying the concept of implicit HCI to a groupware environment for teaching ethics. Pers. Ubiquit. Comput. 1–19 (2021)

Effects of Dietary Similarity on Conversational and Eating Behaviors in Online Commensality

Jui-Ying Wang[1], Sho Kubota[1], Jianpeng Zhanghe[2], and Tomoo Inoue[3]($\boxtimes$) (iD)

[1] Graduate School of Comprehensive Human Sciences, University of Tsukuba, Tsukuba, Japan
[2] Graduate School of Library, Information, and Media Studies,
University of Tsukuba, Tsukuba, Japan
[3] Faculty of Library, Information and Media Science, University of Tsukuba, Tsukuba, Japan
inoue@slis.tsukuba.ac.jp

Abstract. Co-eating, also known as commensality, provides people with an opportunity to chat in a relaxed atmosphere. Research has also suggested some advantages of having food while conversing. In recent years, online commensality, such as remote co-eating via video-calling, has become a way to connect people in different places. However, there are still many people who feel there is a gap between digital and real-life co-eating and consider the interaction in remote co-eating as strange. Besides, there is a lack of studies on the effects of remote co-eating, especially in communication. In this study, we focused on the effects of similarity of meal items and explored how dietary similarity influenced social interaction. We conducted a laboratory-based experiment to investigate whether eating similar meal items in remote conditions has any positive effects on conversation, food intake, and gaze during remote co-eating communication quantitatively. In our preliminary results, different tendencies were found in communication between sessions when eating the same meal items and sessions when eating different meal items.

Keywords: Remote communication · Online commensality · Remote co-eating · Dietary similarity

1 Introduction

Eating together, also called co-eating or commensality, is an important human activity that connects people to each other. In a typical co-eating situation, people share new information about their life, share the taste of food, coordinate their eating pace and amount, have fun, feel relaxed and connected, and share intimacy while eating together [1–7]. In recent years, more people live apart from their family members for several reasons [8] and the COVID-19 lockdown policies have separated many people from their colleagues and friends. Remote co-eating has consequently become a reasonable solution to reconnect people who are physically apart. For example, some companies hold online parties, such as welcome parties and drinking parties, to enhance unity and work efficiency. However, few studies have looked at the effects of remote co-eating;

D. Hernández-Leo et al. (Eds.): CollabTech 2021, LNCS 12856, pp. 20–34, 2021.
https://doi.org/10.1007/978-3-030-85071-5_2

moreover, the survey done by Ceccaldi et al. [1] has suggested that there are still many people who feel that there is a gap between digital and real-life co-eating and consider the interaction in remote co-eating as strange.

In this sense, it is necessary to explore ways to support and achieve remote co-eating communication. To fulfill this purpose, we will continue to analyze conversations, food intake, and gaze during co-eating communication quantitatively to further explore co-eating experience. Studies have found that some of the effects of food on the communication, such as speech, is more equalized when people are provided with food [9], and that overlaps in conversation are less frequent when people can see their partner's plate of food [10]. In this study, we focused on the effects of the similarity of meal items in a remote co-eating situation. In Japanese, there is an expression "eat rice from the same kettle" to mean living under the same roof, implies close relationship. Research has also suggested that people generally consider the person eat similar food as a member of the "same group" and have a more positive attitude toward that person [11, 12]. However, how the similarity of meal items affects co-eating communication has not yet been fully examined and remains unknown. Thus, we were curious about the effects of dietary similarity on co-eating communication.

In this study, a laboratory-based experiment with within-subject design was conducted and the effects of different similarities of meal items were investigated. In our preliminary results, some differences in tendencies were found in communication between the sessions eating the same meal items and sessions eating different meal items.

2 Literature Review

2.1 Co-eating Communication

Co-eating, such as eating together for dinner, teatime, parties, and during a break in a meeting, provides people with an opportunity to share information casually in a relaxed atmosphere. Research to understand communication during co-eating has found some typical patterns and effects in face-to-face co-eating communication. For instance, some actions act as cues for turn-taking in co-eating communication, such as sipping and eye movement [13–15]. For example, Mukawa et al. found that a speaker would look at one of the listeners and show an intention for turn-taking in a three-party co-eating situation. Another person would look at their food to show their intention to avoid being the next speaker [15]. In some cases, conversation would be prioritized over intake, and a person would continue to speak, even with a mouth full of food, after getting a turn-taking cue [16]. Besides, in the aspect of food intake, people also tend to mimic others' intake actions within five seconds [5, 6]. In these co-eating communication studies, conversation, food-intake action, and gaze were found to be important components of social interaction during co-eating.

In the aspect of the effect of having food, Inoue et al. found that the amount of speech was more balanced in face-to-face conversation between three people when they were provided with food than when they were not provided with food [9]. Characteristic patterns in the content of co-eating conversations have also been found, such the participant's feelings about the different conditions, including aspects of hunger, communication, co-eating, and environments, were collected using a 7-point questionnaire and short interviews. As the topic of satiety in family co-eating [17], where the frequency of proposing a new topic was also found to be lower and the frequency of back-channeling higher compared to normal conversations [14]. Besides, Mukawa et al. and Woolley et al. found that using a "large plate" that allows people to share food may also affect their interaction patterns and coordination during and after the meal [10, 18]. To sum up, the existence and format of meals affect face-to-face co-eating communication. However, research on co-eating in remote environments is limited (see Sect. 2.2) [1, 19, 20]. To realize remote co-eating support, it is important to know the actual situation of remote co-eating communication.

2.2 Remote Co-eating

In recent years, the use of information technology to support commensality has been studied. Niewiadomski et al. reviewed works on digital commensality over the past five years in the IEEE Xplore Digital Library, ACM Digital Library, and Appetite. They found researchers originally paid more attention to helping and corrective technologies for cooking and eating, but recently also paid attention to health, well-being, and food experiences in human–food interaction. They divided digital commensality into two kinds: multimodal mixed-reality commensality and artificial commensality [19]. Remote co-eating via video calling, also called tele-dining and Skeating (Skype eating) [20], has become a way to maintain or create connections between individuals via a common technology. Some studies about it have been conducted, but are still rare [1, 19, 20].

Furukawa et al. investigated the effect of the visibility of the meal on communication in three conditions, namely, face-to-face co-eating, remote co-eating where the partner's food can be seen on the screen, and remote co-eating where the partner's food cannot be seen on the screen. The study found that people looked at their partner more frequently in the remote conditions and more overlaps occurred when the meal was not visible [10]. Some studies focused on asynchronous remote co-eating systems and their interaction [21, 22]. However, the understanding of how to support remote co-eating communication and remote co-eating communication itself is still limited and needs more exploration.

2.3 Meal Items

"What do others eat?" is something we may pay attention to in a co-eating scenario, and we also usually compare what others eat with what we eat [3]. Food is considered an individual identity for determining whether people belong to the same group [11, 23]. Some studies have investigated the effect of eating similar meal items as the co-diner. Woolley et al. found that participants who were assigned to eat similar foods trusted each other more and were more cooperative in a labor negotiation game played in an experiment [12]. Further, sharing meal items could produce bonding, increase coordination, and implies a positive/friendly social relationship between co-eaters [2, 4, 18]. While these studies analyzed traditional co-eating in face-to-face situations, we were curious what the effect would be in remote conditions. In addition, since these studies had not focused on communication during the meal, the influence of meal items on communication was not known.

By quantitatively investigating the impact of eating the same meal items on communication in remote co-eating situations, we could examine how to utilize the social functions of commensality, even remotely, and provide design guidelines for remote commensality support.

3 Method

Motivated by the aforementioned gaps and problems, we experimentally investigated the effects of different similarities of meal items in remote co-eating communication. A laboratory-based experiment with within-subjects design was conducted with three conditions, namely, a "same meal item" condition, "different meal item" condition, and "no meal item" condition. To focus on the effects of dietary similarity, this paper only focuses on a comparison of the same and the different meal conditions. Before the experiment was conducted, we were granted ethical approval from our university's IRB, the Research Ethics Review Committee of the University of Tsukuba, Department of Library, Information and Media Studies (No. 20–88).

3.1 Participants

Twelve students aged 21 to 24 years (6 males and 6 females) joined this study voluntarily and were divided into six pairs (pairs A–F). Consistent with previous research, all the pairs were composed of the same gender [5, 15] and were strangers [12] to avoid the inferences of mixed genders or different relationships. Participants were recruited through social networking services and received 500 yen for participating. In addition, due to the limitations of our recruitment, all the participants were international students in Japan who were fluent in Chinese.

3.2 Experiment Design

In this study, a within-subjects design was adopted to remove the effects of personal co-eating communication habits. For that, some people are more talkative or are able to eat more comfortably in front of others, while others are not. To explore the effects of food, three conditions were developed and counterbalanced: the "same meal item" condition where the same meal items were provided to both participants, the "different meal item" condition where different meal items were provided to each participant, and the "no meal item" condition where no meal items were provided. In the experiment, participants attended three remote sessions with the same partner in the three conditions mentioned earlier. In each session, the main activity was to chat freely with the partner in their native language, Chinese, via a video call lasting 10 min. The participants received a paper sheet with a list of chat topics so that they would not run out of topics. They could either talk about the topics listed on the sheet of paper or other topics that came to mind. Because the partner was a stranger of a similar age, the situation was similar to meeting a new friend during a meal or at teatime.

3.3 Meal Items

In the same and the different meal item condition, the participants were provided with meal items. Snacks were adopted as meal items to form different dietary similarities by providing participants with the same or different snacks [12]. To remove the effects of the type of snacks, a total of 18 snacks (see Fig. 1), such as sweets, candies, cookies, potato chips, etc., were prepared and served randomly. These snacks were all common and popular in Japan. We showed the snacks to the participants in the beginning to confirm that they would eat the snacks. If not, the snacks would be chosen randomly again. To maintain the co-eating communication condition over the whole session, we provided enough snacks so that all the snacks could not be eaten during the conversation.

3.4 Environment

The participants in each pair were separated and placed into two different rooms. Each room's experimental environment is shown in Fig. 2. The participants were seated on a chair facing a 42-in. display 90 cm away. A laptop PC was connected to the display, and Zoom was used as the video conferencing system to allow the participants to meet online. A USB web camera with a resolution of 1920 × 1080 was used, and the partner's face and meal items could be seen clearly on the screen (see Fig. 2). Loudspeakers and microphones were used, and the volume of the partner's voice was adjusted to a normal conversational level.

Pair	Sweets provided in same meal item condition	Sweets provided in different meal item condition	
A	16	9	10
B	17	1	10
C	17	16	14
D	4	18	1
E	15	1	7
F	10	6	8

Fig. 1. An image of the snacks provided for each pair.

Fig. 2. Experimental setting (left) and the image of a co-eating partner on the display (right).

3.5 Procedure of the Experiment

The experiment consisted of three sessions and took about 70 min in total. To balance the effects of order, three sessions with different conditions were counterbalanced with six different orders. The following procedure was followed (take the order of conditions as the same meal item condition, the different meal item condition, the no meal item condition as an example):

1. Explain the experiment to the participants in writing and orally, then obtain their signatures on a consent form.
2. Conduct the first remote session.

    a. Let participants have a 10-min remote co-eating communication in the same meal item condition.
    b. Let participants fill in the questionnaire.

3. Conduct the second remote session.

    a. Let participants have a 10-min remote co-eating communication in the different meal item condition.
    b. Let participants fill in the questionnaire.

4. Conduct the third remote session.

    a. Let participants have a 10-min remote communication in the no meal item condition.
    b. Let participants fill in the questionnaire.

5. Conduct a short interview.

4 Data Collection and Analysis

To explore co-eating communication, the participants' conversations, intake, and gaze during the remote communication were collected and analyzed through a video and questionnaire.

The sessions were recorded using two cameras; one in front of the participants to capture their food intake and changes in their gaze, and another placed to capture the entire experimental environment including the conversation partner on the screen as shown in Fig. 2. The screens during the sessions were also recorded by Windows. Besides the video for objective information, a questionnaire and short interview was used to collect subjective feedback. The questionnaire was made up of 38 items that asked the participant's feelings about the different conditions, including aspects of hunger, communication, co-eating, and environments, which was rated with a 7-point Likert scale (1: strongly disagree to 7: strongly agree). It also included a form for free comments, which was followed by a short interview.

The video data of the 10-min videos for each participant in each condition (36 videos about six hours in total) were manually labeled with ELAN, a video analysis tool, and analyzed quantitatively by the three authors and one research assistant. The labels were defined beforehand in a codebook and had been conferenced by all four observers. After labeling, the proportion (%), frequency (times per minute), average length (seconds per time) in the same and different conditions were calculated and compared.

4.1 Conversation

The following items of conversation were analyzed: silence, speech, both in silence, overlap, filler, back-channeling, and laughter [17]. The function "speech recognition silence recognizer" in ELAN was used to distinguish between participants' silence segment and speech segment as a reference. The threshold volume for silence and speech was set between −25 dB and 35 dB relative to the peak RMS. Besides, to avoid errors caused by short pauses in the speech and noise, the threshold length of silence was set as 0.1 s and the threshold length of a speech was set as 0.3 s. After checking the context of conversation, the periods that a candidate did not speak (more than 0.1 s [17, 24]) were labeled as "silence" and the other periods were labeled as "speak." The periods both candidates did not speak were labeled as "both in silence". However, a short pause under 1 s [14] in a single spoken sentence was not considered as "silence." For example, in the sentence "Since it is a nice day… (a pause of 0.8 s) I'd like to go for a walk…," the pause was not considered as "silence."

During the speech period, "overlap," "filler," "back-channeling," and "laughter" were labeled manually according to the context. The overlapping periods of the speaker's utterances were labeled as "overlap," except the overlapping periods of "filler," "back-channeling," and "laughter" that may have been used to show a thinking process, intention to speak, or psychological sympathy [26] while listening. A typical example of a "filler" was "Um…", and typical examples of "back-channeling" were "yeah," "yup," "uh-huh," and "really?" In addition, the periods of laughter were labeled as "laughter." The minimum length of measurement was 0.1 s due to the limitations of the manual resolution.

4.2 Food Intake

The following three items of food intake were analyzed: "chewing" (food in the mouth), "biting" (or putting food into the mouth), and "taking." The two kinds of typical eating processes are shown in Fig. 3. In one, a participant moves their hand from the home position without food, takes the food, then moves their hand toward their mouth, bites or puts the food into their mouth depending on the size of the food, and then starts to chew before swallowing the food. The other is where a participant moves their hand with food from the home position toward their mouth, because some food had been left in the hand from the last bite or the food was just being held absent-mindedly. In the first situation, the "taking" period starts when the hand is moved from the home position to take the food until the first bite, or the food is put into mouth. In the second situation, the "taking" period starts when the hand is moved from the home position until the next bite or the food is put in the mouth. The moment a participant bites or puts the food into their mouth the action was labeled "biting." The periods "food in the mouth" were labeled as "chewing." According to related work, "food in the mouth" shows the intention of food intake instead of talking, but people sometimes still talk with food in their mouth if they get cues for turn-taking [15]. Besides, if a person puts more food in their mouth while chewing, there would be multiple "biting" during a single "chewing" period.

To investigate the phenomenon of the synchronization of food intake actions among co-eaters, the following two items were calculated and analyzed: number of synchronized biting and the total time of synchronized chewing. Referring to related studies [5, 6, 25], we counted biting as synchronized biting when a participant bit or put food into their mouth within 5 s after the partner had bitten or put food into their mouth [5, 6]. We counted the overlapped time of chewing actions as synchronized chewing time [25].

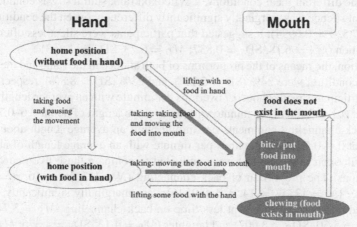

Fig. 3. Process of food intake actions. The colored parts indicate the process, moment, and status labeled as "taking," "biting," and "chewing." (Color figure online)

4.3   Gaze

Participants' gazes were divided into four categories depending on the target of the gaze: "screen," "food," "others," and "unknown". To keep the online gathering natural, no eye-tracking device was used. The gazes were labeled manually according to their head and eye directions in the videos [14, 15]. The periods that a participant looked at the screen were labeled as "screen," whether they were looking at their partner's face or their partner's food, since it was difficult to divide them in the remote condition. The periods that a participant looked at their own food were labeled as "food." The periods that a participant looked at other things, such as a cup, the ceiling, the floor, and the chat topics on the sheet of paper, were labeled "others." If the observer was not able to allocate a target for the gaze of the period, it was labeled "unknown." Further, according to the manual labeling handbook [26], a glance that moves from the original position and back to the same position in a short time without pause, should be labeled as continuing to look at the original position to avoid technical bias.

5 Preliminary Results

5.1 Conversation

The proportion, frequency and average length of the speech labels are as shown in Figs. 4, 5, and 6. Overall, the means of speech proportion in the same and different item conditions were 38% (SD = 11.0%), and 38% (SD = 10.7%), respectively. On average, beyond speaking, participants kept silent for about 60% of the time mainly for listening and eating. The sum of the proportion of speech and silence are not 100% because of the limitations of manual labeling. Besides, participants made 6–7 speech sounds per minute on average, and the average length was 4 s. To compare speech and silence between the same and the different meal conditions, a Wilcoxon rank sum test was conducted. The frequency of silence was marginally significantly different between the conditions ($N = 12$, $W = 17.5$, $p = 0.0994$). It suggested that participants were silent less often in same meal condition ($M_S = 6.18$, $SD_S = 0.837$; $M_D = 6.73$, $SD_D = 1.463$).

In addition, the means of the proportions of both silence in the same and the different meal item condition were 24% (SD = 5.1%), and 23% (SD = 8.8%), respectively. On average, participants made about 0.7 overlaps per minute with an average length of about 0.9 s; about 0.3–0.4 fillers per minute with an average length of about 0.6–0.7 s; about 0.5–0.7 back-channeling comments per minute with an average length about 0.7–0.8 s; and about 0.4–0.5 laughter sounds per minute with an average length of about 0.9–1.2 s. A Wilcoxon rank sum test was conducted to compare these five items between the conditions. The proportion of back-channeling ($N = 12$, $W = 16$, $p = 0.0776$) and laughter ($N = 12$, $W = 14$, $p = 0.0546$) were marginally significantly different. It suggested that participants spent less time on back-channeling ($M_S = 3.74$, $SD_S = 2.615$; $M_D = 5.50$, $SD_D = 3.907$) and laughter ($M_S = 4.13$, $SD_S = 4.376$; $M_D = 5.45$, $SD_D = 3.838$) in the same meal condition, though they were both about 1% of total time.

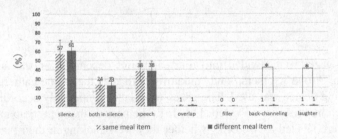

Fig. 4. Proportion of conversational actions.

5.2 Food Intake

The frequency and length of the labeled items in food intake are as shown in Figs. 7, and 8. There is no data for the proportion and average length of a bite because "biting" is an instant action. Overall, the means of proportions of chewing in the same and different item condition were 38% ($SD_S = 29.3\%$) and 34% ($SD_D = 23.2\%$), respectively. The means of the proportion of taking in the same and the different item condition were

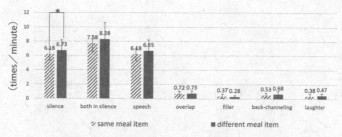

Fig. 5. Frequency of conversational actions.

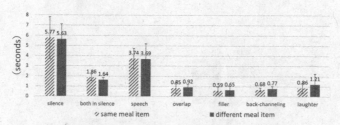

Fig. 6. Average length of conversational actions.

10% (SD_S = 14.5%) and 6% (SD_D = 5.7%), respectively. Generally, the participants seem to spend a little more time taking food and chewing the food in the same meal condition. However, there was no statistically significant difference in the proportion of taking or chewing between the conditions.

On average, participants took and ate the food 1.58 times per minute in the same meal condition (SD_{taking} = 1.439; SD_{biting} = 1.439) and 1.03 times per minute in the different meal condition (SD_{taking} = 0.865; SD_{biting} = 0.880). The length of their taking action was about 2.52 (SD = 1.090) seconds in the same meal condition and 3.85 (SD = 2.276) seconds in the different meal condition. The length of their chewing action was about 31.19 (SD = 17.075) seconds in the same meal condition and 30.50 (SD = 21.055) seconds in the different meal condition. The average time for chewing in both conditions was generally longer because participants sometimes took and ate more food without stopping their chewing. To compare chewing, biting, and taking between the conditions, a Wilcoxon rank sum test was conducted. The average length of taking was significantly different between the conditions (N = 12, W = 11, p = 0.0310). It suggested that participants spent a shorter time taking sweets per time in the same meal condition, in other words, they took and ate sweets more frequently.

The synchronization of food intake actions is as shown in Fig. 9. On average, participants made 3.50 (SD_S = 3.271) and 1.17 (SD_D = 1.427) synchronized bites in the same and different meal conditions. The means of the synchronized chewing time were 117.67 (SD_S = 118.751) seconds and 74.40 (SD_D = 62.220) seconds, respectively, in the same and different meal condition. The means were higher in the same meal condition. However, there was no statistically significant difference in the time for synchronized biting or the time for synchronized chewing between the conditions.

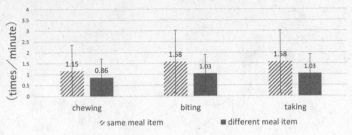

Fig. 7. Frequency of food intake actions.

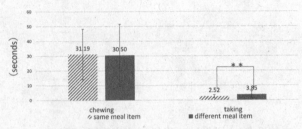

Fig. 8. Average length of food intake actions.

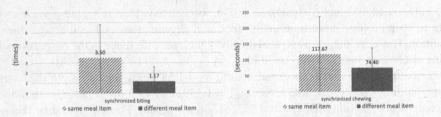

Fig. 9. Number of synchronized biting actions and the total time for the synchronized chewing actions.

5.3 Gaze

The proportion of labeling items for gaze is as shown in Fig. 10. Less than 1% of the targets for gaze were unrecognizable and labeled as unknown. In the same meal condition, the means of the proportion of gazes looking at the screen, food, and other things were 73% (SD = 13.6%), 9% (SD = 6.6%), and 17% (SD = 13.9%), respectively. In the different meal condition, the means of the proportions for screen, food, and other things were 75% (SD = 14.4), 11% (SD = 9.7%), and 13% (SD = 9.5%), respectively. To compare gazes between the conditions, a Wilcoxon rank sum test was conducted. The proportion of gazes at other things was marginally significantly different between the conditions ($N = 12$, $W = 16$, $p = 0.0776$). It suggested that participants in the same meal condition spent more time looking at other things or looked away from the screen and the food for a longer time.

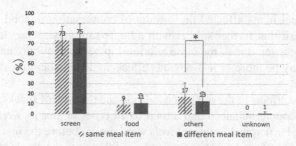

Fig. 10. Proportion of gazes.

6   Discussion

6.1   Speaking and Eating

To explore remote co-eating communication, we analyzed how people speak and eat. According to our preliminary results, participants spent 38% of their time talking on average in both conditions ($SD_S = 11.0\%$, $SD_D = 10.7\%$), and the proportions for having food in their mouth in the same and different meal condition were 38% (SD = 29.3%) and 34% (SD = 23.2%), respectively. We also observed that some participants laughed, made back-channeling comments, or took turns in speaking when there was still food in their mouth to facilitate the conversation. This phenomenon is in line with previous research [15]. According to the 7-point questionnaire, participants somewhat agreed or agreed that it was easy to speak ($M_S = 5.92$, $SD_S = 1.165$; $M_D = 5.42$, $SD_D = 1.240$) and eat ($M_S = 4.92$, $SD_S = 1.975$; $M_D = 5.08$, $SD_D = 1.730$) in a remote co-eating setting. Participants also provided positive feedback on co-eating in the free comments and the interview, for example, "It was easy to have a conversation with food" (B2) and "I was happy to have a conversation while having food" (E1). On the other hand, compared with previous studies that provided participants with curry rice [9, 10], the frequency of speech in this study were lower and the average lengths were longer. The means for frequency of speech were 6.18 ($SD_S = 0.821$) and 6.65 ($SD_D = 1.530$) in this study, and they were between 9–12 in previous studies. The means for average length of speech were 3.74 ($SD_S = 0.997$) and 3.69 ($SD_D = 1.503$) in this study, and they were between 1–2 in previous studies. It shows that the co-eating conversation in this study was at a slower pace. Besides, the proportions of the period no one was talking (both in silence) were 24% ($SD_S = 5.1\%$) and 23% ($SD_D = 8.8\%$) in this study and was 27% in the previous study [9].

To explore the effects of dietary similarity, the study found that the frequency of silence was marginally significantly less in the same meal condition ($N = 12$, $W = 17.5$, $p = 0.0994$), and the average length of taking was significantly shorter in the same meal condition ($N = 12$, $W = 11$, $p = 0.0310$). The results suggest that participants' taking actions were more frequent in the same meal condition. In addition to the shorter average length of taking, the higher mean of frequency was also in line with the finding that the food intake pace was faster in the same meal condition. However, there was no significant difference. Besides, as there was also no significant difference in the proportions of speech or food intake actions in our small sample study, it is still not clear how the meal items affected the amount of conversation or food intake actions. The results suggest that further studies with a larger sample size should be conducted in the future. Moreover, due to the close relationship between culture and eating habits [11, 19], there may be more or less obvious effects in different cultures and these need more exploration.

To remove the effects of the order of condition and the type of snacks, the conditions were conducted counterbalanced and a total of 18 types of snacks were prepared and served randomly. Participants' hunger levels were similar before the first condition with the meal ($M = 3.58$, SD $= 1.782$) and second condition with the meal ($M = 3.75$, SD $= 2.006$), according to the 7-point questionnaire. We observed the pattern of food intake actions with different snack types and gathered some feedback from participants. We found that whether the participants were provided with one-bite snacks or larger snacks, the participants took and ate food more frequently with a shorter average length in the same meal condition, in line with our general findings for food intake.

6.2 Active Conversation During the Meal

In both conditions, participants added some filler and back-channeling comments, and laughter to their conversation. This showed that they were thinking during their conversation and showing some agreement toward their partner. According to the 7-point questionnaire, participants agreed that they understood what partner was saying ($M_S = 6.17$, $SD_S = 0.835$; $M_D = 6.17$, $SD_D = 0.718$) and what they were saying was also understood by their partner ($M_S = 5.83$, $SD_S = 0.937$; $M_D = 5.83$, $SD_D = 0.937$). To explore the effect of meal items, the proportion of back-channeling ($N = 12$, $W = 16$, $p = 0.0776$) and laughter ($N = 12$, $W = 14$, $p = 0.0546$) were marginally significantly lower in the same meal item condition, although the proportions were all about 1% of total time. A previous study suggested that people may make back-channeling comments more frequently instead of showing agreement with normal speech when provided with food [14], but the difference in frequency when provided with same and different food was not clear in this study.

6.3 Gaze

According to our preliminary results, participants spent 73% ($SD_S = 13.6$%) and 75% ($SD_D = 14.4$) of total time looking at screen, 9% ($SD_S = 6.6$%) and 11% ($SD_D = 9.7$%) of total time looking at food and spent 17% ($SD_S = 13.9$%) and 13% ($SD_D = 9.5$%) of time looking of other things respectively in the same and different meal condition. To explore the effect of meal items, the study found that the proportion of gazes looking at other things was marginally significantly higher in the same meal item condition ($N = 12$, $W = 16$, $p = 0.0776$), and there was no significant difference in gazes looking at the screen and food between the same and different meal conditions. Looking at "other things" included looking at specific things and looking away from the screen and food. We observed some of the later type of looking at "other things" when participants were talking. For example, one participant said, "I found someone starts to find a job in ……" (B2) and looked away from the screen when she was thinking what month it was. Besides, in previous studies, gaze was also found to be related to conversation in co-eating as a cue for turn-taking [14, 15]. Our results suggest gaze patterns with speech in remote co-eating should be further explored in the future.

7 Conclusion

In this study, we conducted a laboratory-based experiment, explored communication in remote co-eating, and investigated whether eating similar meal items in the remote condition has any effects on communication. We have provided some quantitative data on conversation, food intake actions, and gaze in the remote co-eating communication. Some preliminary results have shown there were some different tendencies be-tween communication in the same and the different meal condition. The results suggest that there is a chance to constitute a livelier and faster pace of co-eating communication by providing same meal items.

Acknowledgments. This research is financially supported by Nonpi Corporation.

References

1. Ceccaldi, E., Huisman, G., Volpe, G., Mancini, M.: Guess who's coming to dinner? Surveying Digital Commensality During Covid-19 Outbreak. In: Companion Publication of the 2020 International Conference on Multimodal Interaction, pp. 317–321 (2020)
2. Miller, L., Rozin, P., Fiske, A.P.: Food sharing and feeding another person suggest intimacy; two studies of American college students. Eur. J. Soc. Psychol. **28**(3), 423–436 (1998)
3. Cruwys, T., Bevelander, K.E., Hermans, R.C.: Social modeling of eating: a review of when and why social influence affects food intake and choice. Appetite **86**, 3–18 (2015). https://doi.org/10.1016/j.appet.2014.08.035
4. Fischler, C.: Commensality, society, and culture. Soc. Sci. Inf. **50**(3–4), 528–548 (2011)
5. Hermans, R.C., Lichtwarck-Aschoff, A., Bevelander, K.E., Herman, C.P., Larsen, J.K., Engels, R.C.: Mimicry of food intake: the dynamic interplay between eating companions. PLoS ONE **7**(2), e31027 (2012)
6. Sharps, M., et al.: Examining evidence for behavioural mimicry of parental eating by adolescent females. An observational study. Appetite **89**, 56–61 (2015)
7. Chartrand, T.L., Lakin, J.L.: The antecedents and consequences of human behavioral mimicry. Annu. Rev. Psychol. **64**(1), 285–308 (2013)
8. Sellaeg, K., Chapman, G.: Masculinity and food ideals of men who live alone. Appetite **51**, 120–128 (2008)
9. Inoue, T., Otake, M.: Effect of meal in triadic table talk: equalization of speech and gesture between participants. Pap. Hum. Interface Soc. **13**(3), 19–29 (2011). (in Japanese)
10. Furukawa, O., Inoue, T.: Showing meal in video-mediated table talk makes conversation close to face-to-face. Trans. Inf. Process. Soc. Jpn. **54**(1), 266–274 (2013). (in Japanese)
11. Fischler, C.: Food, self and identity. Soc. Sci. Inf. **27**(2), 275–292 (1988)
12. Woolley, K., Fishbach, A.: A recipe for friendship: Similar food consumption promotes trust and cooperation. J. Consum. Psychol. **27**(1), 1–10 (2017)
13. Laurier, E.: Drinking up endings: conversational resources of the café. Lang. Commun. **28**(2), 165–181 (2008)

14. Tokunaga, H., Mukawa, N., Kimura, A., Terai, H.: An analysis of dialog–act structures in three-party table-talk—Evaluation of eating-together communications using gaze-behaviors and dialog–act tags. IEICE Technical report 110(459), HCS2010-68, pp. 55–60 (2011). (in Japanese)
15. Mukawa, N., Minezoe, M., Tokunaga, H., Terai, H., Yuasa, M., Tateyama, K.: Analysis of three-party table talk through gazes, eating-motions and turn-taking behaviors: comparison between platter-for-share-style and individual-plate-style. IEICE Technical report 109(224), HCS2009-51, pp. 17–22 (2009). (in Japanese)
16. Mukawa, N., Tokunaga, H., Yuasa, M., Tsuda, Y., Tateyama, K., Kasamatsu, C.: Analysis on utterance behaviors embedded in eating actions: how are conversations and hand-mouth-motions controlled in three-party table talk? The IEICE Trans. Fundam. Electron Commun. Comput. Sci. (Jpn. Ed.) A **94**(7), 500–508 (2011). (in Japanese)
17. Laurier, E., Sally, W.: Finishing the family meal. The interactional organization of satiety. Appetite **56**(1), 53–64 (2011)
18. Woolley, K., Fishbach, A.: Shared plates, shared minds: consuming from a shared plate promotes cooperation. Psychol. Sci. **30**(4), 541–552 (2019)
19. Niewiadomski, R., Ceccaldi, E., Huisman, G., Volpe, G., Mancini, M.: Computational commensality: from theories to computational models for social food preparation and consumption in HCI. Front. Robot. AI **6**, 119 (2019)
20. Spence, C., Maurizio, M., Huisman, G.: Digital commensality: eating and drinking in the company of technology. Front. Psychol. **10**, 2252 (2019)
21. Nawahdah, M., Inoue, T.: Virtually dining together in time-shifted environment: KIZUNA design. In: Proceedings of the 2013 Conference on Computer-Supported Cooperative Work, pp. 779–788. Association for Computing Machinery, NY (2013)
22. Obata, K., Nakamura, Y., Chen, L., Augeri, J.: Support of making video messages for asynchronous distance co-eating—Adopting personal preferences and randomness for keeping continuous communication. IEICE Technical report 119(190), MVE2019-7, pp. 19–20 (2019). (in Japanese)
23. Polivy, J.: What's that you're eating? Social comparison and eating behavior. J. Eat. Disord. **5**(1), 1–5 (2017)
24. Koiso, H., Horiuchi, Y., Tsutiya, S., Ichikawa, A., Den, Y.: An analysis of turn-taking and back-channels based on prosodic and syntactic features in Japanese map task dialogs. Lang. Speech **41**(3–4), 295–321 (1998)
25. Hirose, N.: Sequential analysis of action disfluencies during lunch. In: The Proceedings of the Annual Convention of the Japanese Psychological Association, vol. 75, p. 2AM091 (2011). (in Japanese)
26. Mizukami, E., Yano, H.: Temporal structure of inter- and intra-speaker's pauses in dialogue. Japanese Society for Artificial Intelligence KENKYOUKAISHIRYOU 39, SIG-SLUD-A302-08, pp. 43–48 (2003). (in Japanese)
27. Hosoma, H., Kohei, K.: Introduction to ELAN, 1st edn. HITUZISYOBOU, Tokyo (2019)

Learning Gains in Pyramid Computer-Supported Collaboration Scripts: Factors and Implications for Design

Ishari Amarasinghe[(⊠)] [ID], Davinia Hernández-Leo [ID], Emily Theophilou [ID],
J. Roberto Sánchez Reina [ID], and René Alejandro Lobo Quintero [ID]

ICT Department, Universitat Pompeu Fabra, Barcelona, Spain
{ishari.amarasinghe,davinia,hernandez,emily.theophilou,
roberto.sanchez,renealejandro.lobo}@upf.edu

Abstract. Computer-Supported Collaborative Learning (CSCL) scripts aim to structure the process of collaboration creating opportunities for productive social interaction and learning. Despite CSCL research has shown these benefits for some scripts in particular contexts, more evidence is needed about to what extent learning gains are actually achieved for more families of scripts and in different conditions of implementation. This paper studies how three CSCL scripts based on the Pyramid collaborative learning flow pattern facilitate students learning in online classes. Learning gains are measured in terms of precision and confusion assessment criteria. Students' behaviour in the learning process, regarding agreement in the knowledge exchange, is also analysed in relation to the learning gains. Results bring out several factors, and implications for the design of fruitful Pyramid scripts implementation, that related to the pedagogical envelope, the type of tasks, pyramid design elements, the need for epistemic orchestration, and debriefing.

Keywords: Computer-Supported Collaborative Learning · Scripts · Collaborative Learning Flow Patterns · Learning gains · Pyramid script

1 Introduction

Free collaboration does not necessarily induce productive interactions among students and therefore does not offer a guarantee of leading to effective learning gains [2]. Directly influencing desired students' interactions by adhering to different strategies, such as using collaborative learning scripts, are seen to enhance students' interactions during collaboration. Collaborative learning scripts prescribe how and when learners may interact, how learner groups require to be formulated, and how learners are required to solve problems together [7, 8]. In other words, scripts structure collaborative learning processes and can be seen as a detailed and explicit contract between teachers and learners [2]. Such guidance becomes important as learners may have a limited understanding of how to interact in collaborative learning situations, to share useful information, to build, and engage in fruitful argumentation [9]. A computational representation of a collaborative

© Springer Nature Switzerland AG 2021
D. Hernández-Leo et al. (Eds.): CollabTech 2021, LNCS 12856, pp. 35–50, 2021.
https://doi.org/10.1007/978-3-030-85071-5_3

learning script forms what is known as a Computer-Supported Collaborative Learning (CSCL) script, that provides opportunities to mediate and guide the implementation of the collaborative learning activities both in in-person and online learning situations.

The notion of Collaborative Learning Flow Patterns (CLFPs) refers to an abstraction of broadly accepted collaboration scripts that structure the flow of collaboration [5]. Some of the well-known examples of CLFPs include Pyramid, Jigsaw, Think-Pair-Share (TPS), and Thinking Aloud Pair Problem Solving (TAPPS) [5]. Through their design rationale, these CLFPs aim to structure collaboration. For instance, the Pyramid CLFP is expected to support learners in reaching an agreed solution for a complex problem that does not usually have a concrete solution [5]. First learners will study a given problem individually to propose an initial solution. Learners then join in small groups, usually in pairs to discuss their solutions, and to propose a shared solution at the small group level. The discussion and negotiation will repeat in growing sizes of groups following a Pyramid structure until the whole group reaches a common solution to the given problem. The design rationale of the script promotes equal participation, knowledge co-construction, and improved negotiation. The Jigsaw CLFP is expected to encourage intensive interactions among students as the completion of the task is not possible without all partners' contributions. The design rationale of the script fosters positive interdependence.

Even though CLFPs and scripts, in general, provide guidance and structure for collaboration, empirical studies that provide evidence to support the claim that scripted collaboration is effective for domain learning are lagging behind [15]. Moreover, how different factors, e.g., the type of task, script design elements, teacher regulation, influence domain learning during scripted collaboration is not fully understood yet. More research is needed to provide evidence of the benefits that scripted collaboration entails in real-learning situations and how such structured collaboration impacts students' learning gains and the related design factors. To this end, the present study aims to generate more evidence in this field by studying how scripted CSCL activities lead to learning gains across three online learning situations scripted according to the Pyramid pattern. The study also contributes with two measurements namely: 1) level of precision and 2) level of confusion that can be used to evaluate learning gains in such CSCL scenarios. Moreover, students' behaviour in the learning process, regarding the agreement with the knowledge exchange, is also analysed in relation to the learning gains. The findings of the study are discussed to shed light on different factors that may have influenced students' learning across the cases and how different factors may lead to implications in the design and implementation of Pyramid scripts. The research question proposed in this study is *"How does the Pyramid script impact students' learning gains?"*.

The rest of the paper is organized as follows. Section 2 explains the methodology followed. Section 3 presents the study results followed by Sect. 4 which provides a discussion of the study findings. The final section provides concluding remarks and future research directions.

2 Methodology

2.1 Collaborative Scripting Tool: PyramidApp

In this study, a tool called PyramidApp was used to design and mediate interactions among students following the Pyramid pattern [12]. The tool implements the macro script structure employed by the Pyramid CLFP and has been used by teachers to implement CSCL activities in different learning situations [13]. The tool provides an authoring space for the teachers where they can design CSCL activities configuring several aspects such as the number of students expected, the number of levels in the Pyramid script, and the duration allocated to different phases of the script (details related to the design decisions of the tool are presented in [11]). Once done with the activity design teachers can generate a unique link to the activity which they can later share with students to enact Pyramid activities in their learning scenarios. The tool also provides a teacher-facing learning analytics dashboard through which teachers can view answers produced by individual students and agreed upon as well students' participation at the group levels [1].

In PyramidApp collaboration among students is structured within several phases. 1) First, students are required to login into the tool and provide an individual answer to the given task. 2) Then students are allocated into small groups ($2 < n < 5$) randomly where they get the opportunity to see the answers submitted by their peers. The tool provides a rating mechanism and a discussion space for students to discuss and rate for the best answers (see Fig. 1). 3) At the end of the small group level, the small groups are merged to formulate larger groups automatically. Within larger groups, students can then view the answers agreed upon at the small group level. Students can further engage in discussions at the larger group level and rate for the best answers to reach a consensus at the end of the activity.

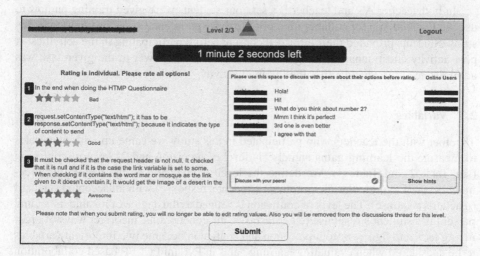

Fig. 1. User interface of the PyramidApp tool (rating space (left), discussion space (right)).

2.2 Contexts and Tasks

Two teachers from the Engineering School of a public university in Spain participated in our study. The design of each collaborative learning activity varied based on the teacher's requirements to conduct CSCL activities in their respective sessions and the time available (see Table 1).

Teacher A deployed two Pyramid scripts in her third-year undergraduate course named "Distributed Applications". One activity was focused on analysing a scenario to identify requirements and in total 25 students (4 female, mean age = 20) took part in these activities. The other activity was related to analysing errors in a computer program and a total of 28 students (4 female, mean age = 20) participated. Teacher A allocated in total 9 min for each Pyramid activity and Pyramids consist of three levels, i.e., option submission level, first rating level, and second rating level. As Pyramid activities were conducted as part of a full-fledged course, before the Pyramid scripts teacher A provided explanations to students about the concepts to be applied in the tasks and how the collaboration activity is connected with what has been taught.

Teacher B deployed a Pyramid activity within the context of an extracurricular workshop on social media. In Teacher B's sessions, 24 first-year undergraduate students (4 female, mean age = 17) participated in the Pyramid activity. As shown in Table 1 teacher B allocated in total 5 min for her Pyramid activity and Pyramids consisted of two levels, i.e., option submission level and a single rating level. The task focused on analysing the effects of digital footprints through a reflection activity based on a fictional scenario. Previous to the Pyramid activity, the students received information about three influencers and their behaviour in social media and had some time to read the information. Following this information they had to identify positive or negative aspects of each influencer and based on their personal judgement they had to select who would be more appropriate for a job position.

In both teacher A's and teacher B's sessions students were given training on how to use the PyramidApp for collaboration prior to the experimental sessions reported in this study. Students provided their informed consent before participating in the activities. A post-activity questionnaire asking students to rewrite an answer to the given task was administered immediately after the Pyramid activity.

2.3 Variables

Together with the teachers who participated in this study we came up with two scales to measure the learning gains namely: 1) level of precision and 2) level of confusion (see Table 2 and Table 3). We define the level of precision as the degree of agreement between a particular measurement (student's response) with an accepted standard (teacher's response). The level of confusion is defined as the degree of misunderstanding present in a student's response (e.g., mistakes, misconceptions, incorrect ways of organizing facts and figures). Both precision and confusion become two important variables to be considered when evaluating learning gains in Pyramid CLFP based collaboration due to a number of reasons. First, in our study both teachers proposed open-ended tasks to students, i.e., there were no simple "yes/no" answers to a given problem but multiple correct solutions and elaborations were possible. In this regard, the level of precision

Table 1. A summary of collaborative learning activities conducted.

Teacher	Scenario	Activity duration	Pyramid levels	No. of students	Task	Educational level
A	1st	9 min	3	25	Determine the non-functional requirements for a scenario of a distributed application	Third year undergraduate students
	2nd	9 min	3	28	Identify errors in software code	Third year undergraduate students
B	3rd	5 min	2	24	Reflect about social media threats in digital footprint scenarios	First year undergraduate students

indicates how far the answers produced by the students align with the teachers' solutions and it also demonstrates the students' knowledge of a particular subject domain [10]. Second, previous studies have shown that pedagogical approaches such as "productive failure" and "confusion" are conductive to learning, as it enables students to learn from their own mistakes [4, 6].

Therefore, it is possible to define the *expectation for CSCL scripts, in terms of learning gains, as an increase in the levels of precision and a decrease in the levels of confusion as a result of the social interaction promoted by the script*. In the case of Pyramid scripts, learning gains are expected to be achieved by a structure that enables students 1) knowledge exchange by contrasting their initial answer to a task with peers' answers leading to socio-cognitive conflicts [14] in contrasting opinions, and 2) knowledge revision by discussing and selecting together the best possible answer.

As a secondary variable, to further understand the learning process happening during the Pyramid script (while refining knowledge based on the knowledge exchange), we also examined the data tracked by the PyramidApp. In particular, we analyse the ratings provided to students' submissions by group members across the pyramid rating levels. It is known that disagreement in collaborative learning can provoke rich argumentation leading to learning [11]. Yet, in the context of factual knowledge tasks, it would be expected that the collaboration process facilitates reconciliation of approaches, and therefore a minimized disagreement by the end of the learning activity. In Pyramid scripts, the expectation would be that in pyramid groups, students would identify confusion and (the most possibly) precise answers in their own and others' submissions, rating accordingly the better submissions in each pyramid level, and therefore advancing in the pyramid flow towards more accurate knowledge. Thus, in this study, a possible expectation is that measures of (dis)agreement could be an indicator of potential learning gains: the more the agreement, the more chances of reaching precise/non-confused answers; the more the disagreement, the more chances for reaching non-precise/confused answers.

Section 3 reports to what extent different designs and implementations of Pyramid scripts are achieving those expectations, in terms of learning gains (precision, confusion) and (dis)agreement measures.

Table 2. Level of precision.

Definition	Measure
Student's response does not match the concepts presented in teacher's answers	0 – Not Precise
Student's response is oriented to the concepts presented in Teacher's response, but it is a lack of consistency	1 – Slightly Precise
Student's response mostly aligns with the concepts presented in Teacher's response	2 – Almost Precise
Student's response matches with the concepts presented in Teacher's response	3 – Precise

Table 3. Level of confusion.

Definition	Measure
Student's response does not present any mistakes, biases, misunderstandings. It fully arranges the given information in his/her explanation or task performance	0 – None
Minor mistakes appear in student's response, but these do not compromise the clarity of his/her explanation or quality in performed tasks	1 – Low
Mid-size mistakes appear in student's response which may compromise his/her answers or performed tasks	2 – Intermediate
Critical mistakes are present in student's response which misguide his/her explanation or performed task	3 – High

2.4 Data Analysis

Statistical analysis was conducted using SPSS software (version 26). The paired-sample t-test or wilcoxon signed rank test was used to report the learning gains based on the distribution (normality) of precision and confusion measures.

To measure disagreement of students' ratings we used standard deviation. For a given group a larger standard deviation indicates a higher disagreement, and a smaller standard deviation indicates a lower disagreement. As there were a number of groups formulated for a given Pyramid rating level, e.g., first rating level and second rating level, we calculated the average standard deviation to represent the disagreement as a whole for a given level.

3 Results

3.1 Learning Gains

As shown in Table 1, the different types of activities considered were: 1) Determine the non-functional requirements for a scenario; 2) Identify errors in software code, and 3) Reflect about social media threats. First, Teacher A and Teacher B evaluated the students' answers for precision and confusion following the scales presented in Table 2 and Table 3. Then they also indicated the learning gains for each student considering the precision and confusion presented in initial and post submissions. In the following, we present the results regarding learning gains for each Pyramid activity conducted.

1st Scenario: Software Engineering Problem: Determine Non-functional Requirements. In Fig. 2(a) and Fig. 2(b) each data point represents students based on the precision and confusion level scores assigned by Teacher A to their initial and post submissions. As shown in Fig. 2(a) the initial answers submitted by 44% of the students were precise (in different levels) but confusion was also present. Data points positioned on the positive X-axis indicates that 32% of the students submitted initial answers with levels of precision and without levels of confusion. Data points in (0,0) position indicate that initial answers submitted by 24% of students were not precise but confusion related elements were also not detected. As shown in Fig. 2(b) when considering the post submissions, it can be seen that 56% of students submitted post submissions that were in general more precise than in the initial submission, but confusion was still also present. 44% of students submitted post submissions with positive levels of precision without levels of confusion.

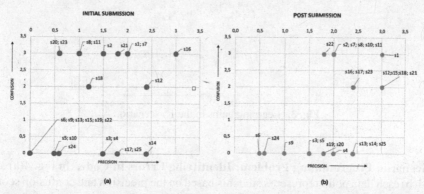

Fig. 2. Precision and confusion: initial submission vs. post submission in the 1st scenario.

In the following we provide a summary of the students' learning gains in terms of precision and confusion (difference between the post submission and the initial submission). In Fig. 3 a data point in red indicates cases without learning gains and green indicate cases with learning gains. The data points in the Q1 quadrant show that 16% of students' answers have an increased precision but also present an increase in confusion. Data points in Q4 quadrant indicate increased precision and decreased confusion in 12% of students' answers. Data points positioned on the positive X-axis also indicate increased precision and zero confusion in 52% of students' answers. Such scenarios, i.e., increased precision and decreased confusion and increased precision and zero confusion in students' answers indicate a clear learning gain (being a total of 64%). A data point in (0,0) position indicates that 16% of students' answers did not indicate a change in precision and confusion. Q3 quadrant indicates decreased precision but also decreased confusion in one students' answer. In terms of levels of precision, post submissions reached a higher average value (M = 2.076; SD = 0.69) when compared to the initial submissions (M = 1.11; SD = 0.89). A paired sample t-test indicated statistically significant differences; t (24) = 5.8, p < .01. Regarding the average levels of confusion, post submissions reached higher average values (M = 1.4; SD = 1.32) when compared to the initial submissions (M = 1.24; SD = 1.45). A wilcoxon signed rank test indicated the difference was not significant; T = 13, z = 0.71, p > .05.

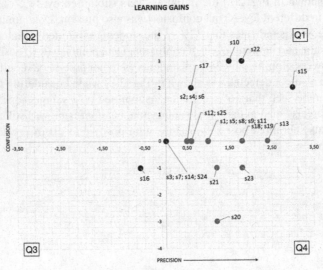

Fig. 3. Learning gains in the 1st scenario.

2nd Scenario: Programming Problem: Identifying Errors in Code. In Fig. 4(a) and Fig. 4(b) each data point represents students based on the precision and confusion scores assigned to their initial and post submissions by Teacher A for a programming problem. As shown in Fig. 4(a) the initial answers submitted by a student (3.6%) consisted of both precision and confusion related elements. Data points positioned on the positive X-axis indicate that 50% of students submitted initial answers with levels of precision and without presenting confusion. Data points in (0,0) position indicate that initial answers submitted by 25% of students were not precise but confusion related elements were also not detected. Data points along the Y-axis indicate that 21.4% of students submitted initial answers that were not precise and included confusion-related elements. As shown in Fig. 4(b), when considering the post submissions, it can be seen that 10.72% of students submitted post submissions that were precise, but confusion was also present. 78.57% of students submitted post submissions that were precise and in those submissions, confusion was not detected. 10.71% students' submitted post submissions that did not indicate a change in precision and confusion.

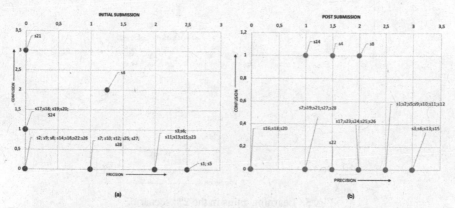

Fig. 4. Precision and confusion: initial submission vs. post submission in the 2nd scenario.

In the following we present a summary of students' learning gains in the 2nd scenario in terms of precision and confusion. In Fig. 5 a data point in red indicates cases without learning gains and green indicates cases with learning gains. The data points in the Q1 quadrant show that 7.14% of students' answers have an increased precision but also present an increase in confusion. The assessment of the teacher clearly indicated that this was a case of confusion propagation in the knowledge revision, where students adopted incorrect knowledge exchanged by another student (about a supposed error in the code that was not such). Data points in the Q4 quadrant indicate increased precision and decreased confusion in 17.86% of students' answers. Data points positioned on the positive X-axis also indicate increased precision and no modification in the level of confusion in 42.86% of students' answers. A data point along the Y-axis indicates that 7.14% of students' answers show a case of no increase in precision but a decreased confusion. Cases including increased precision and decreased confusion, increased precision and no modification in the level of confusion, and no increase in precision but decreased confusion indicate a clear learning gain (being a total of 67.86%). A data point in (0,0) position indicates that 25% of students' answers did not indicate a change in precision and confusion. No data points fall into Q2 and Q3 quadrants. In terms of average levels of precision, the post submissions were more precise (M = 1.80; SD = 0.93) when compared to the initial submissions (M = 0.87; SD = 0.92). A wilcoxon signed rank test indicated that this difference was significant; T = 0, z = 3.86, p < .01. In terms of levels of confusion, post submissions consisted of less confusion (M = 0.11; SD = 0.31) when compared to the initial submissions (M = 0.36; SD = 0.73). A wilcoxon signed rank test indicated the difference was not significant; T = 9, z =1.73, p >.05.

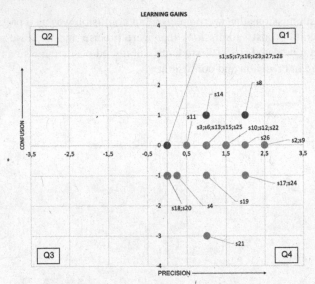

Fig. 5. Learning gains in the 2nd scenario.

3rd Scenario: Reflect About Social Media Threats in Digital Footprint Scenarios.
For the third learning scenario, in Fig. 6(a) and Fig. 6(b) each data point represents
students based on the precision and confusion scores assigned to their initial and post
submissions by Teacher B. As shown in Fig. 6(a) the initial answers submitted by 79.16%
of the students had some level of precision but confusion was also present. A data point
positioned on the positive X-axis indicates that a student (4.17%) submitted an initial
answer that was slightly precise and in the answer, confusion was not detected. Data
points along the Y-axis indicate that initial answers submitted by 16.67% of students
were not precise and confusion related elements were detected.

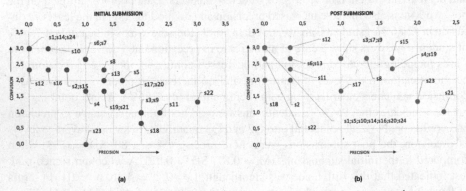

Fig. 6. Precision and confusion: initial submission vs. post submission in the 3rd scenario.

As shown in Fig. 6(b) when considering the post submissions it can be seen that 62.5% of students submitted post submissions that had levels of precision but confusion was also present. Data points along the Y-axis indicate that 37.5% of students submitted post submissions that were not precise and in those submissions, confusion was detected.

In the following a summary of students' learning gains in the 3rd scenario in terms of precision and confusion are presented. In Fig. 7 a data point in red indicates cases without learning gains and green indicate cases with learning gains. The data points in the Q1 quadrant show that 20.83% of students' answers have an increased precision but also present an increase in (propagated) confusion. This scenario presents cases (data points) in the Q2 quadrant, indicating that 37.5% of the students' revised answers presented a decreased precision and increased confusion. Q3 quadrant indicates decreased precision but with decreased confusion in one students' answer (4.16%). Data points in the Q4 quadrant indicate increased precision and decreased confusion in one students' answers (4.16%). Only such cases (in Q4) indicate a clear learning gain (i.e. 4.16%). Data points in (0,0) position indicate that there were no changes in precision nor in confusion in 16.66% of students' answers. Data points positioned on the negative X-axis indicate decreased precision and no changes in confusion in 12.5% of students' answers. A data point positioned on the positive Y-axis indicates no changes in precision but increased levels of confusion in one students' answer (4.16%). Finally, in terms of average levels of precision the post submissions were less precise (M = 0.68; SD = 0.75) when compared to the initial submissions (M = 1.15; SD = 0.81). A paired sample t-test indicated significant differences; t(23) = -2.2, p < .05. In terms of confusion, post submissions presented more average levels of confusion (M = 2.52; SD = 0.56) when compared to the confusion presented in initial submissions (M = 1.93; SD = 0.81). A paired sample t-test indicated that this difference was significant; t(23) = 4.3, p < .01.

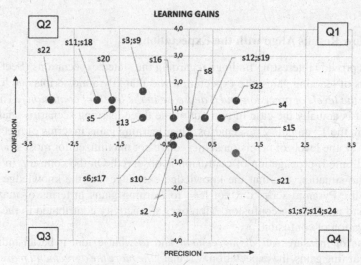

Fig. 7. Learning gains in the 3rd scenario.

3.2 (Dis)agreement Measures in Ratings Across the Collaborative Learning Flow

As mentioned before (see Table 1) teacher A conducted Pyramid activities with two rating levels and Teacher B conducted a Pyramid activity with one rating level. As shown in Fig. 8 in teacher A's class in general the disagreement seems to decrease in the second rating level showing that students are reaching an agreement as the Pyramids evolve in time. In teacher B's class disagreement was observed for the first rating level of the Pyramid activity. As there was no second rating level in this class, we couldn't compare the differences of the level of disagreement across Pyramid levels in this case.

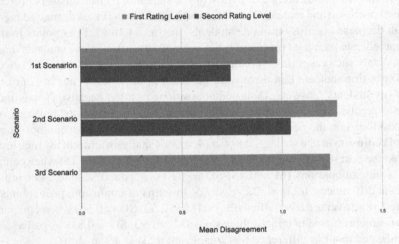

Fig. 8. Disagreement during Pyramid activities.

3.3 On How Results Align with the Expectations

The results provide interesting findings regarding the stated expectations (Sect. 2.3).

In terms of learning gains, the expectation was that "Pyramid scripts can lead to *an increase in the levels of precision and a decrease in the levels of confusion*". The results show that it is actually the case in two out of the three learning scenarios analysed. In particular, in the 1st and the 2nd scenarios, clear learning gains in terms of precision are observed. Yet, the levels of precision achieved are not maximized for most students and some (but limited) propagation of confusion is observed. On the contrary, in the third scenario, the situation was that the knowledge exchange and the knowledge revision guided by the Pyramid script did not lead to learning gains in terms of maximizing precision and minimizing confusion. Moreover, the activity contributed to the creation and propagation of confusion.

In terms of measures of *(dis)agreement* and to what extent it be an indicator of potential learning gains, the expectation was that "*the more the agreement, more chances reaching precise/non-confused answers; the more the disagreement, the more chances for reaching non-precise/confused answers*". As summarised in Fig. 8 during the 1st scenario and 2nd scenario the disagreement became low in the second rating level of the Pyramid script. Moreover, as commented above in the 1st and the 2nd scenarios clear learning gains in terms of precision are observed. These results suggest that the study findings are in alignment with our expectations that a high agreement creates more chances to reach precise/non-confused answers. Moreover, the disagreement observed within the first rating level of the Pyramid script in the 3rd scenario can be interpreted as a lower level of agreement creates chances to reach non-precise/confused answers.

The next section discusses how these results suggest that several factors may affect the potential learning gains facilitated by these scripts and implications for the design of Pyramid scripts implementation.

4 Discussion: Factors and Implications for Design and Implementation

The present study aimed to analyse how scripted Pyramid CSCL activities could lead to learning gains across three different online learning scenarios. Overall findings suggest that scripted CSCL activities can enhance learning outcomes although the precision and confusion in learning gains may depend on teaching scenarios and mediating factors. In our consideration, factors such as the pedagogical envelope, the type of tasks, pyramid design elements, the need for epistemic orchestration and debriefing may have influenced the design and implementation of the examined Pyramid activities. The following section discusses how factors may have affected the results of the study.

4.1 The Pedagogical Envelope: Prior Activities

As observed in the data analysis, learning outcomes in the designed activities varied from class to class. Results obtained from Teacher B's class activity may suggest contrary expected outputs. Nevertheless, it is important to observe the nature of the activities and the prior experience of students with the explored topic. Teacher A's activities were part of a formal lesson and therefore students were familiar with the class and the teaching materials. Conversely, Teacher B's activity occurred in an extracurricular environment. Enrolled students were not asked for any prior preparation, and the activity was used as an ice breaker activity to encourage students to meet each other.

4.2 The Type of Task

The results of the study indicated that the type of task can have an impact on the students' learning gains in these scripted learning situations. Precision and confusion in post submissions varied in all developed tasks (1st scenario and 2nd scenario showed more precision and less confusion while 3rd scenario showed less precision and more confusion). Although confusion is propagated in all tasks, results show that openness of the task might lead to major confusion. Teaching activities in 1st scenario and 2nd scenario presented more answer-oriented exercises in contrast to 3rd scenario which demanded dealing with assumptions based on previous experiences and personal opinions. Although open-ended tasks can be given to students with the expectation that tasks will create an opportunity for students to negotiate and co-construct a solution, current study findings show that these types of tasks require careful consideration and intervention of teachers to achieve the intended learning outcomes.

4.3 Pyramid Design Elements: Pyramid Levels

Pyramid flow design elements may have also had an impact on the findings. In comparison to the two rating level activities, single rating level activity may have not provided opportunities for students to revise their knowledge in the process of reaching an agreement. As observed in the analysis, the level of disagreement between students tended to decrease with the increasing levels of group phases of the Pyramid script. Post submissions in the 1st scenario and 2nd scenarios, where Pyramid activities consisted of two rating levels showed increased precision whereas the 3rd scenario in which Pyramid activity consisted of a single rating level did not produce significant learning gains. These findings are aligned with the findings of previous similar research [14].

4.4 The Need for Teacher Intervention: Epistemic Orchestration

Another possible explanation for the results can be connected to the role of the teacher in monitoring the scenario. Teachers' intervention is essential to mediate cases where top levels of precision are not achieved, and confusion occurs so that confusion related elements do not propagate to the subsequent levels of the activity. Commonly referred to as *orchestration* in these types of learning situations teachers are required to manage collaboration in real-time [3]. Teachers not only have to regulate students' participation in groups, but they also need to constantly evaluate the content produced by students that can also be described as epistemic orchestration of the learning activity. This could be supported, for example, by learning analytics tools such as teacher-facing dashboards, through which they can monitor a large number of groups simultaneously, and embedded warning mechanisms that alert teachers automatically to the relevant indicators [1]. These indicators could include the presence of confusion, decreased precision in students' answers, and increased disagreement that can facilitate their epistemic orchestration, overall contributing to establish a fruitful collaborative learning climate.

4.5 Pedagogical Envelope: The Need for Teacher-Led Debriefing

Connected to the preceding idea, a suitable intervention by the teacher during the learning scenarios have a potential influence on the learning gains. Teacher-led debriefing activities at the end of learning activities can contribute to reflect on the conflicting points with the whole class. Noted confusing elements in students' answers can be discussed at the end of the activity with the whole class by the teacher [4]. Teacher-facing dashboards can assist teachers in flagging answers consist of confusing elements that require discussion at the individual, group, or whole class level.

5 Conclusions and Future Work

This paper aimed to explore how Pyramid pattern-based learning scripts impact student's learning gains. The findings of the study have shown that the observed differences in the learning gains at three different cases can be interpreted by referring to a number of different factors: the pedagogical envelope; the type of task; Pyramid design elements;

the need for teacher intervention and need for teacher-led debriefing. Moreover, based on the improved precision observed in students' post submissions it is evident that the particular Pyramid pattern-based CSCL activities conducted using the PyramidApp facilitate learning. However, the aforementioned factors require careful consideration.

There are several limitations of this study. First, the number of cases we considered is low and with each case representing a different task for collaboration. The number of students participated in each activity is relatively low and the prior activities they engaged in are different across the cases. Although teachers who participated in the study agreed precision and confusion as valid measurements to evaluate learning gains, the precision and confusion assigned to students' answers are strictly dependent on the teacher's personal judgement. The above limitations can have an impact on the obtained learning gains. However, the exploration of these factors needs to be acknowledged as an important contribution of our work. In the future, we are planning to explore further how some of these design elements, specifically the teachers' aspects related to epistemic orchestration and teacher-led debriefing, can influence the precision and confusion presented in students' answers and therefore learning gains. Moreover, in the future, it is also important to extend a more detailed analysis of the student's behaviour during the learning process (e.g., chat discussion) to further understand relevant indicators (such as (dis)agreement measures) of potential learning gains.

Acknowledgements. This work has been partially funded by the Volkswagen Foundation (COURAGE project, no. 95567). TIDE-UPF also acknowledges the support by FEDER, the National Research Agency of the Spanish Ministry, TIN2017-85179-C3-3-R, PID2020-112584RB-C33, MDM-2015-0502 and by ICREA under the ICREA Academia programme (D. Hernández-Leo, Serra Hunter).

References

1. Amarasinghe, I., Hernández-Leo, D., Michos, K., Vujovic, M.: An actionable orchestration dashboard to enhance collaboration in the classroom. IEEE Trans. Learn. Technol. **13**(4), 662–675 (2020)
2. Dillenbourg, P.: Over-scripting CSCL: the risks of blending collaborative learning with instructional design. In: Kirschner, P.A. (ed.) Inaugural Address, Three Worlds of CSCL. Can We Support CSCL? pp. 61–91. Open Universiteit Nederland, Heerlen (2002)
3. Dillenbourg, P.: Design for classroom orchestration. Comput. Educ. **69**(1), 485–492 (2013)
4. D'Mello, S., Lehman, B., Pekrun, R., Graesser, A.: Confusion can be beneficial for learing. Learn. Instr. **29**, 153–170 (2014)
5. Hernández-Leo, D., Villasclaras-Fernández, E.D., Asensio-Pérez, J.I., Dimitriadis, Y.A., Retalis, S.: CSCL scripting patterns: hierarchical relationships and applicability. In: 6th IEEE International Conference on Advanced Learning Technologies, pp. 388–392 (2006)
6. Kapur, M.: Productive failure in learning math. Cogn. Sci. **38**(5), 1008–1022 (2014)
7. Kollar, I., Fischer, F., Hesse, F.W.: Collaboration scripts - a conceptual analysis. Educ. Psychol. Rev. **18**(2), 159–185 (2006)
8. Kobbe, L., et al.: Specifying computer-supported collaboration scripts. Int. J. Comput. Support. Collab. Learn. **2**(2–3), 211–224 (2007)

9. Liu, L., Hao, J., von Davier, A.A., Kyllonen, P., Zapata-Rivera, J.D.: A tough nut to crack: measuring collaborative problem solving. In: Handbook of Research on Technology Tools for Real-World Skill Development (2016)
10. Loibl, K., Roll, I., Rummel, N.: Towards a theory of when and how problem solving followed by instruction supports learning. Educ. Psychol. Rev. **29**(4), 693–715 (2017)
11. Malzahn, N., Aprin, F., Hoppe, U., Eimler, S., Moder, S.: Measures of disagreement in learning groups as a basis for identifying and discussing controversial judgements. In: Proceedings of the 14th International Conference on Computer-Supported Collaborative Learning, pp. 233–236 (2021)
12. Manathunga, K., Hernández-Leo, D.: Authoring and enactment of mobile pyramid-based collaborative learning activities. Br. J. Edu. Technol. **49**(2), 262–275 (2018)
13. Manathunga, K., Hernández-Leo, D.: Flexible CSCL orchestration technology: mechanisms for elasticity and dynamism in pyramid script flows. In: Proceedings of the 13th International Conference on Computer Supported Collaborative Learning, pp. 248–255 (2019)
14. Mugny, G., Doise, W.: Socio-cognitive conflict and structure of individual and collective performances. Eur. J. Soc. Psychol. **8**(2), 181–192 (1978)
15. Radkowitsch, A., Vogel, F., Fischer, F.: Good for learning, bad for motivation? A meta-analysis on the effects of computer-supported collaboration scripts. Int. J. Comput. Support. Collab. Learn. **15**(1), 5–47 (2020). https://doi.org/10.1007/s11412-020-09316-4

Emotion Annotation of Music: A Citizen Science Approach

Nicolás Felipe Gutiérrez Páez(✉)⬤, Juan Sebastián Gómez-Cañón⬤,
Lorenzo Porcaro⬤, Patricia Santos⬤, Davinia Hernández-Leo⬤,
and Emilia Gómez⬤

Universitat Pompeu Fabra, Barcelona 08005, Spain
{nicolas.gutierrez,juansebastian.gomez,lorenzo.porcaro,
patricia.santos,davinia.hernandez-leo,emilia.gomez}@upf.edu

Abstract. The understanding of the emotions in music has motivated
research across diverse areas of knowledge for decades. In the field of
computer science, there is a particular interest in developing algorithms
to "predict" the emotions in music perceived by or induced to a listener.
However, the gathering of reliable "ground truth" data for modeling the
emotional content of music poses challenges, since tasks related with
annotations of emotions are time consuming, expensive and cognitively
demanding due to its inherent subjectivity and its cross-disciplinary
nature. Citizen science projects have proven to be a useful approach
to solve these types of problems where there is a need for recruiting
collaborators for massive scale tasks. We developed a platform for annotating emotional content in musical pieces following a citizen science
approach, to benefit not only the researchers, who benefit from the generated dataset, but also the volunteers, who are engaged to collaborate on
the research project, not only by providing annotations but also through
their self and community-awareness about the emotional perception of
the music. Likewise, gamification mechanisms motivate the participants
to explore and discover new music based on the emotional content. Preliminary user evaluations showed that the platform design is in line with
the motivations of the general public, and that the citizen science approach offers an iterative refinement to enhance the quantity and quality
of contributions by involving volunteers in the design process. The usability of the platform was acceptable, although some of the features require
improvements.

Keywords: Citizen science · Crowdsourcing · Collaborative
annotation · Music Emotion Recognition · Motivations

1 Introduction

Citizen science has been defined as the participation of different audiences in scientific research, specifically to gather, submit or analyze large quantities of data
[8]. The increase of citizen science projects in recent years is attributed to the

© Springer Nature Switzerland AG 2021
D. Hernández-Leo et al. (Eds.): CollabTech 2021, LNCS 12856, pp. 51–66, 2021.
https://doi.org/10.1007/978-3-030-85071-5_4

developments in information science, data informatics, graphical user interfaces and system-based web applications, as well as the refinement of the strategies for retaining volunteers and the methods for assuring data quality [19,48]. Citizen science projects that are entirely mediated by information and communication technologies are often considered a form of crowdsourcing applied to science [47]. Yet, crowdsourcing is considered the most basic level of the participatory research approaches, and it is necessary to increase public involvement in the research process to enhance the benefits for both researchers and citizens [18,21]. Crowdsourcing has been used in different research fields to collect, analyze and process data. Platforms such as Amazon Mechanical Turk[1] or Prolific[2] are widely used to recruit experiment participants and or collaborators for massive scale tasks such as image annotation, classification or content analysis by offering tangible rewards in the form of monetary compensation. Other platforms such as Zooniverse[3] focus on participants' intrinsic motivation (e.g., to have fun or to gain knowledge) to engage people in such tasks. In the field of music, there are several crowdsourcing initiatives to engage public participation.

One of the principal reasons why people engage and interact with music is emotion [16] - songs produce goosebumps and chills, evoke inner feelings, or provoke particular memories. This has motivated research across diverse areas of knowledge for decades: music cognition [14,26,27], philosophy [12], musicology [13], neuroscience [35], and computer science [4,42,49]. In the latter, there is a particular interest in developing algorithms that could "predict" the emotions in music perceived by or induced to a listener – known as the field of music emotion recognition (MER). Nevertheless, the gathering and study of reliable "ground truth" data for modeling the emotional content of music pose challenges, since tasks related with annotations of emotions in music are time consuming, tedious, and expensive [2], as well as cognitively demanding due to its inherent subjectivity and its cross-disciplinary nature [29]. Several studies have collected emotion annotations in music through human annotation following different approaches. On the one hand, traditional surveys provide a straightforward technique for collecting information about emotional content in music [16], but the required costs in terms of human resources, time and money reduces the chances to fully share the gathered data within the research community [29]. On the other hand, collaborative online games have been designed for the collection of music data, such as MajorMiner [33], Listen Game [43], TagATune [31], MoodSwings [28] or Emotify [3]. Even when this approach seems to engage volunteers, some studies have suggested that certain participants may perceive gamification as a trivialization of the research objects, or can demotivate participants with lower scores or low contribution rates [7,41].

The aim of this work is to present the iterative process followed for the design of a platform to collect emotion annotations in music. This work follows a citizen science approach and explores different mechanisms for engaging participation.

---

[1] https://www.mturk.com/.

[2] https://www.prolific.co/.

[3] https://www.zooniverse.org/.

The outline of this document is as follows. In Sect. 2 we present the platform requirements definitions for both researchers and volunteers, and the importance of participants' motivations in the design process. Section 3 provides an overview of the designed platform and the theoretical background that support the design decisions. Section 4 describes the preliminary results obtained from different user evaluation testing scenarios and Sect. 5 describes the conclusions and future directions.

2 Platform Design Requirements

2.1 "Ground Truth" Data for MER

In the context of MER, there are different representations of emotions, supported by a large body of music cognition research [15,22,26,29]. These representations are categorized in two taxonomies: categorical/discrete [17] and dimensional/continuous [40]. In discrete/categorical models, a defined set of basic emotional descriptors (tags) is used to describe the emotions in music. Examples of such models are basic emotions (e.g., such as happy or sad) or clusters of emotional adjectives like those created for the Music Information Retrieval Evaluation eXchange (MIREX) audio mood classification task [23]. Dimensional models suggest that emotions can be scaled and measured by a continuum of descriptors or simpler multidimensional metrics, such as the circumplex model of affect (i.e., arousal refers to energy/activation, and valence relates to pleasantness/positiveness of an emotion) [40]. Both categories have been extensively studied and compared, and results suggest that even when there are clear methodological differences, there is a high correspondence between the discrete and dimensional models [14–16]. However, both approaches present drawbacks. In fact, the categorical/discrete approach is naturally ambiguous to describe rich human emotions, while the dimensional/continuous approach makes the mapping of a particular emotion to arousal-valence space vague and unreliable. Thus, it is important to provide different layers of annotation (from free-text to concise classes of emotions) in order to produce enriched, multi-level datasets. Additionally, recent research [20,24] has shown impact of inter-rater agreement of the emotional content in music on the performance of MER systems, hence there is a need to better understand how agreement is achieved in different layers of annotation.

R1. *Annotations should follow different representations emotions to better understand the agreement among annotators (inter-rater agreement) and to obtain results that can be compared and/or integrated to other available datasets.*

Another important aspect to consider from the theoretical and methodological points of view is the distinction between perceived and induced emotions [6]. Perceived emotions refer to those recognized by the listener when interpreting musical properties (music can communicate qualities associated with emotions)

[27]. Induced or felt emotions involve psycho-physiological responses to music (emotional response to music of the listener) [30]. The challenge for annotators is the common confusion between both of these concepts, adding a layer of complexity to the annotation process.

R2. *Annotations should include information to identify whether the listener response is based on the judgement of perceived or induced emotions.*

In addition to the emotion annotation, it is of special interest to identify participants' factors that have some influence on the behavior/preference of the annotators in emotion annotation [42]. These factors may include spoken languages, birthplace, current mood, familiarity with music and their preference for the music excerpt.

R3. *Annotations should include individual characteristics of the listener, and the context in which the annotation was generated.*

2.2   Citizen Science Approach for Collaborators' Recruitment

As it was mentioned before, the problem of generating "ground truth" data for MER can be tackled from the perspective of citizen science. According to the four level categorization proposed by Haklay [21] for citizen science initiatives, this project falls in the category of distributed intelligence, since participants are asked to take basic training and then collect data or carry out data interpretation.

R4. *Training material and tutorials must be designed in order to gather quality annotations. Likewise, the designed platform should support participants' learning beyond the initial training.*

R5. *The designed platform should foster collaborations between researchers and communities, as well as to promote self-reflection and awareness regarding the research in MER.*

In citizen science research, the understanding of participants' motivations to contribute has a special relevance for projects' sustainability [25,34,37,39]. Even when these studies follow different motivation theories, their results highlight the importance for project organisers to determine the motivations they may wish to appeal through the project tasks, and that it should be also noted that not all motivations will be catered for within each project [45,46].

R6. *The designed platform should implement different incentive mechanisms to engage contributions from participants with different short and long-term motivations.*

One of the issues raised from the implementation of citizen science is regarding data sharing to allow others to build on completed work, and to foster debate and critical feedback [38]. In order for a citizen science project to produce outcomes that impact the research field, the information and data generated should be made publicly accessible in a timely manner and in a suitable form for multiple uses [9].

R7. *The designed platform should follow open science principles to make analysis and results of collected data public. To do this, data within the platform needs to conform as much as possible to existing data and process standards, and data privacy must be ensured for participants personal information.*

3   Platform Description

The Music Enthusiasts (ME) web platform was designed to fulfill the identified requirements. The platform allows participants to annotate the perceived emotions in different music pieces, following circumplex model of affect and providing basic and GEMS [50] emotion tags for each quadrant. Participants can compare their annotations with the community results, and receive musical recommendations based on the provided annotations. They also have training material to understand the goals of the research and how to contribute with their annotations according to the differences between evoked and perceived emotions. Likewise, the prototype implements gamification mechanisms (scoring systems, rankings and rewards) to engage participants to contribute. Besides, researchers can create different annotation tasks (campaigns) within the platform. Each campaign consists of a determined number of songs to be annotated, and participants can choose in which campaign they want to participate. Furthermore, the platform was translated into English and Spanish. This section describes the relevant aspects of the ME platform.

3.1   Definition of the Annotation Task

In order to gather annotations and implement **R1**, a hybrid multi-level representation of emotions was selected. As shown in Fig. 1, the core of the annotation is composed of three main sections. The first two sections collect ratings of the perceived arousal (low or high) and valence (negative or positive). To reduce the complexity and as an attempt to improve the inter-rater agreement, the annotation task only gathers binary information about arousal and valence. In this layer of annotation, we produce distinct classes from the annotations depending on the combination of arousal and valence dimensions. Thus, every annotation is mapped into one of the four quadrants of the dimensional taxonomy. The second part is a discrete tag of emotion corresponding to the specified quadrant. Eleven discrete emotion tags from the basic and the GEMS model are used, namely joy, surprise, power (quadrant 1: positive arousal and valence), anger, fear, tension (quadrant 2: positive arousal and negative valence), sadness, bitterness (quadrant 3: negative arousal and valence), peace, tenderness and transcendence (quadrant 1: negative arousal and positive valence).

To implement **R2** each annotation also includes free-text fields for explaining the reasons behind each choice. The implementation of **R3** is divided into three parts. As shown in part (C) of Fig. 1, a first set of individual characteristics is collected during the annotation task. The platform stores a binary indication of the annotator's familiarity with and preference for the excerpt, as well

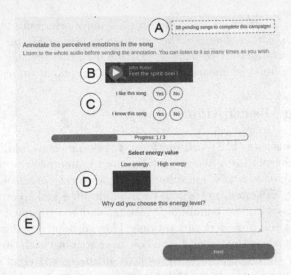

Fig. 1. Annotation interface. (A) Indicator with the number of pending songs within the campaign. (B) Music player. Participants must click on play to start listening. (C) Participants indicate if they are familiar with the song and if they like/dislike it. (D) Core of the annotation. It has three steps: arousal, valence and a discrete emotion tag (Only arousal is shown in this image). (E) Participants can add their reasons for each of their choices.

as the timestamp of the annotation. The second part is collected previous to an annotation. Participants report their current mood through a free-text field and a force-choice using the Pick-A-Mood tool [44]. The participant's mood report is only asked after six hours of the last report (Fig. 2a). The third part of the individual characteristics is collected when users register in the platform (Fig. 2b). This information is anonymized and participants have full control over the shared information (i.e., following the implementation of **R7**). They can modify or delete their information from the platform at any time they wish. Internally, the ME platform links each annotation with a unique identifier associated to the user. This is the only field that external researchers have to link contextual information with the emotion annotation.

3.2 Motivations and Incentive Mechanisms

This research follows the motivational model proposed and evaluated by Nov et al. [34], in which participants' motivations to contribute in a citizen science project are categorized as collective motives (importance attributed to the collective goals of the project), reward motives (potential benefits to be gained from participation, such as reputation or social interaction), norm-oriented motives (expected reactions of important others such as family and friends) and intrinsic motives.

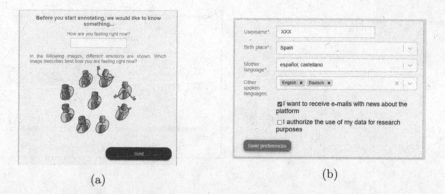

(a)   (b)

Fig. 2. Individual characteristics gathering. (a) Mood selection screen. (b) Participants are the owners of their own personal data, and they can modify, erase or add information at any time. This process only affects the available contextual information associated to the user, but not the collected emotion annotations.

In order to implement **R4**, **R5** and **R6**, the ME platform includes intrinsic and extrinsic incentives for users to participate in the community (Fig. 3). The platform is designed to be promoted as a platform to get recommendations based on emotional content (external reward). After completing five annotations, participants receive a musical recommendation that is stored in their profiles, creating customized playlists that can be accessed at any time. Likewise, the promotion and the information and text within the platform is designed to highlight the importance of every contribution to the research in Music Emotion Recognition (collective motives). Participants are also engaged to contribute to gain knowledge about how certain musical features relate with the emotional content in music, and to understand the wisdom of crowds and how other community members perceive music (social interaction and performance improvement). A feedback dashboard is presented to the participants after completing an annotation, so they are able to compare their perceptions with the community, to foster self-reflection and social learning. Gamification mechanisms such as a scoring system based on output-agreement, user progress statistics (number of annotations provided, number of campaigns completed) and ranking systems (fun, social interaction and public recognition) are also included.

3.3   Contributor Environment

The ME platform has been developed in the context of TROMPA (Towards Richer Online Music Public-domain Archives) project. To implement R6, the data infrastructure of the ME platform is centered around the TROMPA Contributor Environment (CE), which is a web-based platform that interlinks items hosted within different music repositories. The CE is implemented as a graph database that does not incorporate the content itself, but it refers to content hosted in web-accessible public repositories using URIs [32]. Thus, the annota-

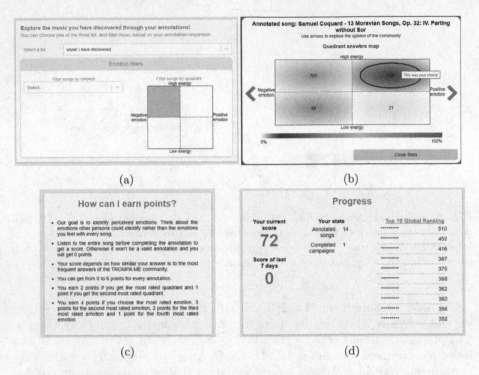

Fig. 3. Incentive mechanisms. (a) My Musical profile section. Participants can explore the annotated music as well as the recommended music at any time, and apply filters based on the community results or on the MER algorithms trained with the available data. (b) Participants receive feedback of their performance compared with the community responses (output-agreement mechanism) (c) Participants can access the scoring system information at any time. Based on their responses and how close they are to the previously obtained annotations, participants receive 0 to 6 points. (d) Progress dashboard. It includes the user position within the community, number of annotations/campaigns completed and a global ranking based on the scoring system.

tions generated through the ME are stored following the Web Annotation Data Model[4] as generic core representation, which enables annotations to be shared and reused across different hardware and software platforms. Additionally, all the annotations can be linked to the anonymized information of the participant who generated the annotation. The user information is stored either in the ME's database or in the users' decentralized data stores (Pods). Thus, users keep control of their information and can unlink or remove their information at any time, without affecting the emotion annotation.

---

[4] https://www.w3.org/TR/annotation-model.

3.4   A Framework to Assess Outcomes and Usefulness of the Incentives

The impact of a citizen science project can be measured in terms of research out-comes (quantity of results, quality of results), participation outcomes (including sustained participation in time) and learning outcomes (knowledge exchange between citizens and researchers) [1]. We propose to collect data from different sources: questionnaires about usability and participants' perceptions, data logs to analyze participants' behavior within the community (number of annotations, number of registered users, average time spent in annotation tasks, analysis of navigation paths within the platform, etc.), and the results of annotations' anal-ysis in the context of MER. These sources of information will allow us to obtain real time feedback about the outcomes of the project, and to create a collabo-rative environment between researchers and citizens to refine the ME platform.

4   User Evaluation and Results

4.1   Evaluation Study

The platform has been tested in a controlled online study. The objective of this study was to evaluate the functionality and usability of the ME platform, deter-mine the effectiveness of the incentives created within the platform and evaluate compliance with the design requirements. We created three campaigns of choral music within the platform, to be completed by the participants. Participants worked individually to complete the assigned tasks. The duration of the study was approximately two hours distributed over several days, and the content of the material was made available in Spanish and English. The study was divided into two phases. During the first phase, participants completed seven tasks (explore the *Home* section, explore the *About us* section, register in the platform, edit their user profile, annotate all the songs of a campaign, explore the annota-tion feedback, explore the recommended music). Participants self-assessed their ability to complete the tasks (*Did you complete the requested task?*), answered single-choice questions to validate their understanding of different concepts and mechanisms within the platform (the dimensional taxonomy, the scoring system usage, and the reward system usage), and answered Likert-scale questions to self-report their motivations to participate (Table 1). During the second phase, participants were requested to complete a long annotation campaign (60 songs) during several days (spending in total around 1 h). For evaluating the usability of the system we applied the System Usability Scale (SUS) test, which has been widely used and proved to be a reliable instrument [10,11].

A total of 21 participants (11 male, 10 female) with an average age of 26 years old (rank = 12) participated in the evaluation study. All the participants self-reported they were able to complete the requested tasks, and we verified completion using the platform log. Regarding the understanding of concepts and mechanisms, 19 participants (90.5%) understood the reward system, but only 14 (66.7%) fully understood the descriptors used to classify the music

Table 1. Likert-scale questions to self-report participants' motivations. Adapted from Nov et al. [34].

Code	Question
KNO	I want to learn about musical properties and the emotions associated with them
FUN	I want to have fun while I discover new music based on its emotional content
REP	I like to compete with other users
SOI	I like to be able to compare my results with other users
COM	I want to help in this project for the automatic recognition of emotions in music

(e.g., arousal, valence, evoked emotions, perceived emotions) and 11 participants (52.4%) understood the scoring system and the feedback. Regarding the participants' motivations (Fig. 4), have fun while discovering music based on its emotional content (FUN) and learn about musical properties and the emotions associated with them (KNO) were the best rated motivators, followed by altruist motives (COM). On the other hand, the scoring system and the community feedback (REP, SOI) had the lowest rating. Regarding the usability, the average SUS score was 72.9/100 (SD = 8.8, rank = 35). Usability and Learnability scores had similar values to the general SUS score (71.6 and 74.2 respectively).

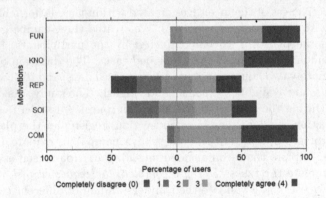

Fig. 4. Self-reported motivations to contribute in tasks for emotion annotation of music.

These results suggested that the information within the platform was not sufficient as training material, and the explanation of the scoring system was not clear enough. To tackle these issues some refinements were implemented within the platform: the different annotation fields were merged into one single screen to make participants aware of their choices at any time during the annotation task (Fig. 5a). Additionally, a new field was added to the annotation to collect a free-text tag of the most salient emotion perceived within the excerpt in the native language of the participant, adding a new level of emotion annotation to the fixed categories for each musical excerpt and consistent with research from neuroscience [5]. Predefined options were added as suggestions for the free-text fields for explaining the reasons behind each choice. Moreover, a help button was added in the annotation section, so the participants could access a detailed explanation of how to complete the annotation task and how the scoring and reward systems works (Fig. 5b). Furthermore, the platform was translated into two additional languages (Italian and Dutch) to reach a higher audience.

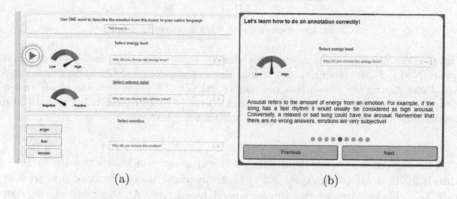

(a)   (b)

Fig. 5. Platform refinements. (a) Annotation fields were merged into one single screen. (b) New help menu added during the annotation tasks. This menu is mandatory for the first annotation of new users or users with no recent annotations, and can be accessed by any user in the annotation section.

4.2 Evaluation in Real Conditions

After the refinements, the ME platform was released[5] and three different engagement campaigns were executed: a first contest with two external rewards for the top contributors (29th of June to 5th of July 2020), a second contest with three additional external rewards for the top contributors and for volunteers who completed an usability survey (14th to 20th of October 2020) and a long promotion campaign without external rewards (January 2021). Regarding the usability, the average SUS score was $72.9/100$ (SD $= 13.8$, rank $= 47.5$). The results of the t-test showed that there is no significant differences between the results from the version used in the evaluation study and the results in real conditions ($t = 0.003$, $p\text{-}value > 0.05$). Additionally, participants were asked about their perception regarding the music they discovered through the platform (Fig. 6), and results suggest that participants discovered completely new music when annotating (DM1) since most of it was music that they do not tend to listen (REC1). Still, the recommendations require refinement to make them more appealing for participants (DM2, REC2).

---

[5] https://enthusiasts.trompamusic.eu/.

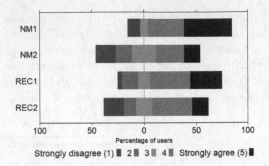

Fig. 6. Perception of users about the musical recommendation and the discovered music. **NM1:** *I discovered new music using this application.* **NM2:** *I found new music that I like during the annotation campaigns.* **REC1:** *I thought that the music recommendations received were distant from what I usually listen to.* **REC2:** *I would like to receive music recommendations more in line with my taste*

The log data recorded from the platform usage was extracted (from 1st of March 2020, until 1st of April 2021) to analyze the users behavior and to evaluate the effectiveness of the implemented incentives. At the time of the data

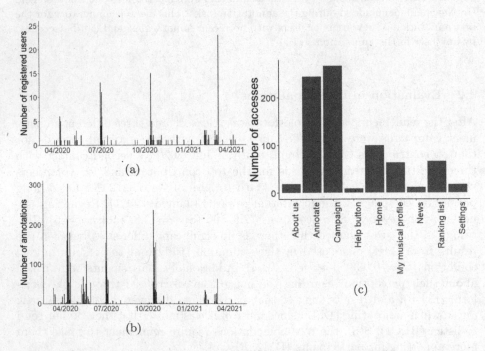

Fig. 7. Partial results of log data analysis. (a) Number of registered users over time. (b) Number of generated annotations over time. (c) Platform modules' accesses count.

extraction, there were 189 registered users and there were 3556 annotations. As it can be seen, both campaigns with external rewards had a significant impact in the number of registered users (Fig. 7a) and the generated annotations (Fig. 7b). Additionally, the users' navigation data (Fig. 7c) suggest that users do not use the help after the first mandatory display. Likewise, they do not tend to access their user settings. Furthermore, the musical reward (music recommendation) and the rankings have similar accesses, suggesting that participants main motivation is to have fun. The reliability of the collected data using Krippendorff's coefficient α was measured to understand the importance of inter-rater agreement on the collected annotations. In summary, we obtained: (1) Arousal = 0.505, (2) Valence = 0.364, and (3) Emotion = 0.192. Despite the low agreement obtained in the annotations (which is consistent with previous studies [4, 20, 24]), this motivates to use the fine-grained annotations (i.e., free-text) produced in this study to develop more personalized and context-sensitive MER applications [49].

5 Conclusions

The developed platform supports the collaborative gathering of "ground truth" data for MER algorithms, while engaging participants in the tasks by providing learning in the research field, self and community-awareness about the emotional perception of the music, and implementing gamification mechanisms (scoring systems, rankings and rewards). The results of the preliminary tests indicate that contributors have intrinsic motivations to participate, i.e., they enjoy discovering new music and want to learn about the emotional content in music while contributing to the project. During the first months of deployment, tangible rewards worked as a strong motivator to engage new users in the platform. Nevertheless, according to the participants motivations, other incentives such as the recommendation system or the gamification mechanisms should be refined in order to provide long term motivation, and to provide a better landing page to make the project goals and the expected outcomes clearer (for both, volunteers and researchers). These required refinements are in line with the usability results, since the ME platform is in the range of "acceptable" applications (72.9 points over 100), and with the analysis made to the platform log data. Concerning the inter-rater agreement, the preliminary analysis shows low agreement, compared with other similar projects, but it is noteworthy that neither the individual characteristics nor the free-text field to explain participants' choices have been yet analyzed. Further analysis will include assessment of participants understanding of emotional representations and the difference between perceived and evoked. Likewise, the platform log data should include users' time line, similar to the ones proposed by Ponciano and Brasileiro [36] to define participants' engagement profiles and refine the incentive mechanisms.

Acknowledgments. This work has been partially funded by the TROMPA project, European Union's Horizon 2020 research and innovation programme under grant agreement no. 770376. TIDE-UPF also acknowledges the support by FEDER, the National

Research Agency of the Spanish Ministry of Science and Innovation, TIN2017-85179-C3-3-R, PID2020-112584RB-C33, MDM-2015-0502, the Ramon y Cajal programme (P. Santos) and by ICREA under the ICREA Academia programme (D. Hernández-Leo, Serra Hunter).

References

1. Abu Amsha, O., Schneider, D.K., Fernandez-Marquez, J.L., Da Costa, J., Fuchs, B., Kloetzer, L.: Data analytics in citizen cyberscience: evaluating participant learning and engagement with analytics. Hum. Comput. **3**(1), 69–97 (2016). https://doi.org/10.15346/hc.v3i1.5
2. von Ahn, L.: Games with a purpose. Computer **39**(6), 92–94 (2006). https://doi.org/10.1109/MC.2006.196
3. Aljanaki, A., Wiering, F., Veltkamp, R.C.: Studying emotion induced by music through a crowdsourcing game. Inf. Process. Manage. **52**(1), 115–128 (2016). https://doi.org/10.1016/j.ipm.2015.03.004. emotion and Sentiment in Social and Expressive Media
4. Aljanaki, A., Yang, Y.H., Soleymani, M.: Developing a benchmark for emotional analysis of music. PLoS One 1–22 (2017)
5. Barrett, L.F.: How emotions are made: the secret life of the brain. Houghton Mifflin Harcourt (2017)
6. Barthet, M., Fazekas, G., Sandler, M.: Music emotion recognition: from content-to context-based models. In: From Sounds to Music and Emotions, pp. 228–252. Springer, Heidelberg (2013). https://doi.org/10.1007/978-3-642-41248-6_13
7. Baruch, A., May, A., Yu, D.: The motivations, enablers and barriers for voluntary participation in an online crowdsourcing platform. Comput. Hum. Behav. **64**, 923–931 (2016). https://doi.org/10.1016/j.chb.2016.07.039
8. Bonney, R., Phillips, T.B., Ballard, H.L., Enck, J.W.: Can citizen science enhance public understanding of science? Public Understand. Sci. **25**(1), 2–16 (2016). https://doi.org/10.1177/0963662515607406. pMID: 26445860
9. Brenton, P., von Gavel, S., Vogel, E., Lecoq, M.E.: Technology infrastructure for citizen science, pp. 63–80. UCL Press (2018). http://www.jstor.org/stable/j.ctv550cf2.12
10. Brooke, J.: SUS - a quick and dirty usability scale. In: Jordan, P.W., Thomas, B., McClelland, I.L., Weerdmeester, B. (eds.) Usability Evaluation in Industry, pp. 189–194 (1996)
11. Brooke, J.: Sus: a retrospective. J. Usability Stud. **8**(2), 29–40 (2013)
12. Budd, M.: Music and the Emotion. Routledge, London (1992)
13. Cook, N.: Beyond the Score - Music as performance. Oxford University Press, Oxford (2013)
14. Eerola, T.: Music and emotions. In: Bader, R. (ed.) Springer Handbook of Systematic Musicology. SH, pp. 539–554. Springer, Heidelberg (2018). https://doi.org/10.1007/978-3-662-55004-5_29
15. Eerola, T., Vuoskoski, J.K.: A comparison of the discrete and dimensional models of emotion in music. Psychol. Music **39**(1), 18–49 (2011). https://doi.org/10.1177/0305735610362821
16. Eerola, T., Vuoskoski, J.K.: A review of music and emotion studies: approaches, emotion models, and stimuli. Music Percept. Interdiscipl. J. **30**(3), 307–340 (2013)
17. Ekman, P.: Are there basic emotions. Psychol. Rev. **99**(3), 550–553 (1992)

18. English, P., Richardson, M., Garzón-Galvis, C.: From crowdsourcing to extreme citizen science: Participatory research for environmental health. Ann. Rev. Public Health **39**(1), 335–350 (2018). https://doi.org/10.1146/annurev-publhealth-040617-013702. pMID: 29608871

19. Science Europe: Science Europe briefing paper on citizen science (2018). https://www.scienceeurope.org/media/gjze3dv4/se_briefingpaper_citizenscience.pdf

20. Gómez-Cañón, J.S., Cano, E., Herrera, P., Gómez, E.: In: Joyful for you and tender for us: the influence of individual characteristics and language on emotion labeling and classification, pp. 853–860. Montréal, Canada (2020)

21. Haklay, M.: Citizen science and volunteered geographic information: overview and typology of participation. In: Sui, D., Elwood, S., Goodchild, M. (eds.) Crowdsourcing Geographic Knowledge: Volunteered Geographic Information (VGI) in Theory and Practice, pp. 105–122. Springer, Dordrecht (2013). https://doi.org/10.1007/978-94-007-4587-2_7

22. Hallam, S., Cross, I., Thaut, M.: The Oxford Handbook of Music Psychology. Oxford University Press, Oxford (2016)

23. Hu, X., Downie, S., Laurier, C., Bay, M., Ehmann, A.: The 2007 mirex audio mood classification task: lessons learned. In: Proceedings 9th International Conference Music Information Retrieval, pp. 462–467 (2008)

24. Hu, X., Yang, Y.H.: Cross-dataset and cross-cultural music mood prediction: a case on Western and Chinese Pop songs. IEEE Trans. Affect. Comput. **8**(2), 228–240 (2017)

25. Jennett, C., Cox, A.L.: Digital citizen science and the motivations of volunteers. In: The Wiley Handbook of Human Computer Interaction, vol. chap. 39, pp. 831–841. Wiley, Hoboken (2018). https://doi.org/10.1002/9781118976005.ch39

26. Juslin, P.N.: Handbook of Music and Emotion: Theory, Research Applications. Oxford University Press, Oxford (2010)

27. Juslin, P.N.: Musical Emotions Explained. Oxford University Press, Oxford (2019)

28. Kim, Y.E., Schmidt, E.M., Emelle, L.: Moodswings: a collaborative game for music mood label collection. ISMIR **8**, 231–236 (2008)

29. Kim, Y.E., Schmidt, E.M., Migneco, R., Morton, B.G., Richardson, P., Scott, J., Speck, J.A., Turnbull, D.: Music emotion recognition: a state of the art review. Proc. ISMIR **86**, 937–952 (2010)

30. Krumhansl, C.L.: An exploratory study of musical emotions and psychophysiology. Canadian J. Exp. Psychol. Revue canadienne de psychologie expérimentale **51**(4), 336 (1997)

31. Law, E.L., Von Ahn, L., Dannenberg, R.B., Crawford, M.: Tagatune: a game for music and sound annotation. In: ISMIR. vol. 3, p. 2 (2007). http://citeseerx.ist.psu.edu/viewdoc/summary?doi=10.1.1.106.7184

32. Weigl, D., et al.: Interweaving and enriching digital music collections for scholarship, performance, and enjoyment. In: 6th International Conference on Digital Libraries for Musicology, pp. 84–88. DLfM 2019, Association for Computing Machinery, New York (2019). https://doi.org/10.1145/3358664.3358666

33. Mandel, M.I., Ellis, D.P.: A web-based game for collecting music metadata. J. New Music Res. **37**(2), 151–165 (2008). https://doi.org/10.1080/09298210802479300

34. Nov, O., Arazy, O., Anderson, D.: Scientists@home: what drives the quantity and quality of online citizen science participation? PLoS One **9**(4), 1–11 (2014). https://doi.org/10.1371/journal.pone.0090375

35. Patel, A.D.: Music as a transformative technology of the mind: an update. In: Honing, H. (ed.) The Origins of Musicality, p. chap. 5. MIT Press, Massachusetts (2018)

36. Ponciano, L., Brasileiro, F.: Finding volunteers' engagement profiles in human computation for citizen science projects. Hum. Comput. **1**(2), 1–17 (2014). https://doi.org/10.15346/hc.v1i2.12

37. Raddick, M.J., et al.: Galaxy zoo: motivations of citizen scientists. Astronomy Educ. Rev. **12**(1),(2013). https://doi.org/10.3847/AER2011021

38. Resnik, D.B., Elliott, K.C., Miller, A.K.: A framework for addressing ethical issues in citizen science. Environ. Sci. Poli. **54**, 475–481 (2015). https://doi.org/10.1016/j.envsci.2015.05.008

39. Rotman, D., Hammock, J., Preece, J., Hansen, D., Boston, C., Bowser, A., He, Y.: Motivations affecting initial and long-term participation in citizen science projects in three countries. In: iconference, pp. 110–124. Presented at the (2014). https://doi.org/10.9776/14054

40. Russell, J.A.: A circumplex model of affect. Personality Soc. Psychol. **39**(6), 1161–1178 (1980)

41. Simperl, E., Reeves, N., Phethean, C., Lynes, T., Tinati, R.: Is virtual citizen science a game? Trans. Soc. Comput. **1**(2) (2018). https://doi.org/10.1145/3209960

42. Soleymani, M., et al.: In: Emotional analysis of music: a comparison of methods, vol. MM 2014, pp. 1161–1164. Association for Computing Machinery, New York (2014). https://doi.org/10.1145/2647868.2655019

43. Turnbull, D., Liu, R., Barrington, L., Lanc kriet, G.R. : A game-based approach for collecting semantic annotations of music. ISMIR. **7**, 535–538 (2007)

44. Vastenburg, M., Romero Herrera, N., Van Bel, D., Desmet, P.: Pmri: development of a pictorial mood reporting instrument. In: CHI 2011 Extended Abstracts on Human Factors in Computing Systems, pp. 2155–2160. CHI EA 2011, Association for Computing Machinery, New York (2011). https://doi.org/10.1145/1979742.1979933

45. Wald, D.M., Longo, J., Dobell, A.R.: Design principles for engaging and retaining virtual citizen scientists. Conserv. Biol. **30**(3), 562–570 (2016). https://doi.org/10.1111/cobi.12627

46. West, S.E., Pateman, R.M.: Recruiting and retaining participants in citizen science: what can be learned from the volunteering literature? Citizen Sci. Theory Pract. **1**(2),(2016). https://doi.org/10.5334/cstp.8

47. Wiggins, A., Crowston, K.: From conservation to crowdsourcing: a typology of citizen science. In: 2011 44th Hawaii International Conference on System Sciences, pp. 1–10 (2011). https://doi.org/10.1109/HICSS.2011.207

48. Wynn, J.: Citizen Science in the Digital Age: Rhetoric, Science, and Public Engagement. The University of Alabama Press, Tuscaloosa (2019)

49. Yang, Y.H., Chen, H.H.: Music Emotion Recognition. CRC Press, Boca Raton (2011)

50. Zentner, M., Grandjean, D., Scherer, K.R.: Emotions evoked by the sound of music: characterization, classification, and measurement. Emotion **8**(4), 494 (2008). https://doi.org/10.1037/1528-3542.8.4.494

Using Network Analysis to Characterize Participation and Interaction in a Citizen Science Online Community

Ishari Amarasinghe[1]([✉]) [ID], Sven Manske[2] [ID], H. Ulrich Hoppe[2] [ID],
Patricia Santos[1] [ID], and Davinia Hernández-Leo[1] [ID]

[1] ICT Department, Universitat Pompeu Fabra, Barcelona, Spain
{ishari.amarasinghe,patricia.santos,davinia.hernandez-leo}@upf.edu
[2] RIAS Institute, Duisburg, Germany
{sm,uh}@rias-institute.eu

Abstract. Citizen Science (CS) projects provide a space for collaboration among scientists and the general public as a basis for making joint scientific discoveries. Analysis of existing datasets from CS projects can broaden our understanding of how different stakeholder groups interact and contribute to the joint achievements. To this end, we have collected publicly available forum data from the "Chimp&See" project hosted on the Zooniverse platform via crawling its *Talk* pages. The collected data were then analysed using Social Network Analysis (SNA) and Epistemic Network Analysis (ENA) techniques. The results obtained shed light on the participation and collaboration patterns of different stakeholder groups within discussion forums of the "Chimp&See" project.

Keywords: Citizen science · Discussion forums · Social Network Analysis · Epistemic Network Analysis

1 Introduction

"Citizen Science" (CS) is a growing trend that builds on the participation of persons not considered as professional scientists in scientific activities and achievements. Although in some areas of science we may still see individual contributions, CS is essentially collaborative and in many cases also interdisciplinary. Often the collaborative activities take place in online communities and make use of different types of collaboration technologies. Accordingly, we see CS as a very interesting subject for research in the area of collaboration technologies.

As summarised and discussed by Haklay et al. [10], there is a huge variety of different and competing definitions of CS. In this spectrum, we find a specific contrast between approaches using citizen science as a means to enhance and support "official" science through crowd-sourcing activities as opposed to grassroots initiatives driven by the volunteers, i.e. the citizen scientists, themselves. We accept that all these manifestations belong to the reality of CS.

D. Hernández-Leo et al. (Eds.): CollabTech 2021, LNCS 12856, pp. 67–82, 2021.
https://doi.org/10.1007/978-3-030-85071-5_5

Accordingly, the quality of scientific output in terms of research results and publications as well as the personal growth, learning and enrichment on the part of the volunteers should be considered as equally valid goals.

Scientometric or bibliometric methods can be applied to CS projects to measure scientific quality based on publications. Kullenberg and Kasperowski [15] have conducted such an analysis with a focus on biology and environmental studies as prominent areas of CS activities. Their analysis also shows the overlaps between the concepts of CS, crowdsourcing and public engagement.

Our focus is on the participation and collaboration patterns that are characteristic for the contributions of volunteers in online CS projects. Emerging technologies are influencing the scientific research process by streamlining data collection in CS, improving data management, expediting communication, etc. [18] In particularly, social networking is enhancing the dialog between scientists and citizen scientists via virtual forums and communities, increasing the collective capital [7]. As indicated by Newman et al. [18] the success of such approaches is dependent on diverse stakeholders' contributions. In order to understand better the phenomenology of CS forums, important questions to be explored are: Which kinds of roles and interactions can we observe and ascertain? Are the volunteers in a way instrumentalised as a kind of "mechanical turks" or do they engage in "legitimate peripheral participation" [16] as a source of learning and personal growth? Aristeidou et al. [1] have studied profiles and levels of engagement on the part of volunteers in CS projects relying on behavioural data from the underlying collaboration platforms. The indicators and metrics used in that study are based on duration measures and counts of certain activity types. In contrast, Huang at el. [14] have used discourse-analytic techniques to study the dynamics of interactions in two CS projects dealing with local environmental problems.

The work reported here has been conducted in the context of the European research project CS Track[1]. One of the cornerstones of CS Track's approach to monitoring and analysing CS projects and activities is the computational analysis of web-based sources. In the case study described here, we use publicly available forum data from the Zooniverse platform[2]. Zooniverse is one of the world's largest CS platforms that invites the public to participate in scientific data analysis and engage in discussions with professional scientists [23]. In our analysis of these data we go beyond a counting/aggregating approach by applying network analysis techniques of two different types: Social interactions and communication in the forum are converted into actor-actor networks using a social network analysis approach [25]. Social network analysis reveals relational structures and possibly role patterns in these communities [13]. In our analysis, we also consider the dynamics of network measures (namely eigenvector centrality) over time, which can indicate if an actor moves from a peripheral to a more central position in the network. In addition to these social relations, we use the approach of "Epistemic Network Analysis" [20] to characterise forum interactions in terms of certain

---

[1] CS Track project: https://cstrack.eu. Retrieved: 2021-04-26.
[2] Zooniverse: https://www.zooniverse.org. Retrieved: 2021-04-26.

types of knowledge building and exchange. Overall, this study is of explorative nature. The guiding aim is to identify (or not) forms of participation that would indicate the taking over of initiative and responsibility by the volunteers in the example project.

2 Analysis Methods

2.1 Social Network Analysis

Originating from the idea of using network or graph models to model social relationships, Social Network Analysis (SNA) provides a rich set of mathematically based analysis techniques, which have been applied in social science and economy studies [5]. SNA methods are frequently used for determining the importance or influence of actors in networked communities based on centrality measures or to determine subnetworks of particularly high connectivity to identify specific subcommunities. The most basic centrality measure is the number of links (and thus neighbours) associated to a given node (degree) whereas closeness or betweenness centralities require the analysis of paths in the overall network. Eigenvector centrality [3] is a recursive version of degree that does not only consider the number of neighbours but again their "weight", which corresponds to the Page rank measure for web search [6]. According to Hollenbeck and Jamieson, such operationalisations using centrality measures can support recruiting and teamwork for the purpose of developing of human capital [12].

Computer-mediated communication activities can be interpreted by SNA techniques in many different ways, always starting from taking certain communication actions as indicators (such as sending a message from A to B) as basic links in a network structure. In discussion forums, "replying" and "mentioning" can be conceived as two basic mechanisms that establish relations between actors. The example to be elaborated on originates from a discussion forum in the context of crowd-sourced citizen science activities.

Networks with directed edges or links allow for considering the directivity of interactions, which is often important in discourse analyses. Here, we would distinguish indegree and outdegree are measures to represent the quantitative involvement of an actor in the discourse. While the outdegree states how many times an actor actively contributed to a discussion in relation to a receiving actor (reply or mention), the in-degree quantifies the receptive characteristics of an actor, namely how many times the actor has been addressed or referred to.

Data. In this study, we extracted data from a discussion forum which is known as "Talk" page of the Chimp&See project hosted on the Zooniverse platform of CS projects. The talk pages are categorised into 3 main categories namely: 1) Help Boards; 2) Chat Boards; and 3) Science Boards. Each board constitutes a number of sub boards that serve as a space for specific discussions between scientists and non-scientists. For instance, there are 4 sub boards under the Help Board namely: 1) Announcements; 2) Frequently Asked Questions (FAQs); 3)

Technical Support; and 4) The Objects. Likewise, the Science Board consists of 22 sub boards and the Chat Board consists of 6 sub boards[3]. Each sub board consisted of a number of conversations (e.g., around 490 conversations in Help Board, around 500 conversations in Chat Board, more than 2000 conversations in Science Board) and each conversation consisted of several posts.

To evaluate and analyse the discourse, all the conversations and posts have been retrieved using a crawling approach. This section describes the data format and metadata that has been stored by the crawler. In addition, the communication in the whole Chimp&See talk pages is modelled as a social network. Following section describes the rules of the network extraction from the forum data, particularly regarding the construction of edges and the assignment of edge weights. The whole process of the data collection consists of the (a) crawling of the Zooniverse talk pages, (b) the extraction of the discourse dataset, (c) and the construction of the social networks. The whole dataset consists of 3218 forum conversations with 24531 individual posts. The forum involved a total of 575 unique user accounts, which represents 10.1% of all the active volunteers of the Chimp& See project. The number of accounts splits up in the following (system) roles: 8 moderators, 25 scientists, 542 volunteers. The time span of the data is from 2015/04/07 to 2019/05/12. Table 1 describes the collected discourse dataset.

Table 1. Description of the dataset

Board category	The specific forum and sub-forum (i.e., the board), e.g. "Chat Board/The Objects/", or "Help Board/Announcements/"
Post number	Sequential post id
Title	Title of the conversation
User type	Moderator—Scientist—User ('Volunteer')—Team ('Zooniverse admin') [0..n]
User	Name of the user who contributed, mostly pseudonyms
Response to	(OPT) Name of the user replying to in the post. A reply is determined by the use of the "reply" button on a specific post.
References to users	(OPT) Mentioning a user within a post text using the '@' sign. [0..n]
References to objects	(OPT) Mentioning an object within a post text using the '@' sign. [0..n]
Timestamp	Time of the post in the format "dd.mm.yyyy hh:mm:ss" , e.g. "31.10.2018 20:35:00"
Post content	Textual representation of the post content. Special markup has been removed
URL	URL of the conversation
Full HTML	Raw HTML of the post

---

[3] Chimp& See Talk Pages: https://talk.chimpandsee.org. Retrieved: 2021-04-10.

Network Extraction. The network for the discourse in the Chimp& See talk pages is modelled as an weighted, directed graph. The set of nodes contains a unique node for each user who contributed to the discussion by creating a post in a conversation. The prescribed role of moderators, scientists and volunteers is modeled as a node attribute. An edge (u, v) is created if one of two conditions is satisfied:

- Reply: if u responds to v explicitly by using the reply functionality of the forum, an edge (u, v) is created
- Reference: if u references v by using the @ notation ('@v') within the message body of the post, (u, v) is created.

Each edge (u, v) is assigned an edge weight w_{uv} which represents the number of references and replies from u to v. Each node a is assigned a node weight v_a, which quantifies the number of contributions (i.e. posts/replies) from user a. As a side note, a post does not necessarily lead to establishing an edge. This is specifically the case if there is no interaction with a user (no replies), thus the degree centrality of such a node can still be zero. For the purpose of visualizing the data with Gephi [2] the particular node weight is multiplied with 100.

The dataset has been partitioned by board category (help, science and chat) to better distinguish the different kinds of communication. In addition, the communication has been sliced into four time slices, whereas each time slice has the span of one year. Due to this partitioning of the data into time slices, a "drop out" occurs in this context when a user does not post anything in subsequent time windows.

2.2 Epistemic Network Analysis

ENA is a novel co-temporal technique that takes into account the temporality in discourse data which avoids limitations of classical coding-and-counting approaches in modeling social interactions over time [8,20]. Different elements present in discourse, e.g., knowledge, skills, communication, that can be labelled following a pre-specified coding scheme is used in ENA to generate weighted dynamic network models that visualise the structure of connections among codes in discourse [20]. ENA has been used to model discourse in different domains such as education and health care [8,21]. However, we are unaware of studies that use ENA to analyse discussions in CS project forums although it has a great potential to model how different user roles, i.e., volunteers, moderators, and scientists interact within such discussion spaces. Hence, in this study, we applied ENA to model, visualise, and quantitatively compare the potential differences in the discussion participation across user roles to broaden our knowledge regarding their collective knowledge building processes.

In ENA network models, the nodes represent the codes and the edges reflect the relative frequency of co-occurrences between codes. In these weighted network models, thicker edges indicate that connections occur more often and thinner edges represent less frequent connections [20]. As ENA positions nodes in a fixed location in the projection space, it enables a visual comparison of different networks. Further, this technique enables to generate difference networks that could highlight salient differences between two networks [20].

Data. As ENA requires the coding of the datasets we had to limit the number of posts considered in this study to an amount that is manageable for manual coding. At the same time, we wanted to select a subset that represents all three types of discussion boards. To this end, first, we randomly selected three sub boards for a given discussion board. Then for a given sub board we again randomly selected three conversations. Then an analysis of the distribution of the posts under each conversation was performed to identify which conversations will be selected for ENA. It was seen that the number of posts under conversations ranged from 2 to 40. To acquire a sufficient number of posts to investigate co-occurrences and to remove any bias resulting from the unequal distribution of the posts for a given conversation we selected conversations that included posts within the range of 10–20 resulting in a manageable, relevant dataset of 130 posts. Table 2 provides a summary of the conversations selected for ENA and the total number of posts included under a given conversation.

Codebook. We followed a bottom-up approach for data coding [9]. After several iterations we came up with a coding scheme that consisted of nine different codes (see Table 3) that are also in alignment with the activities proposed in CS literature [4]. Two authors of this study coded the dataset, any disagreements were resolved by discussion.

Table 2. Conversations selected for manual coding

Board	Sub board	Conversation	Number of posts
Help	Announcements	Chimp&See's 3rd anniversary: Meet the neighbours of the "Ngogo chimps"	13
	Frequently Asked Questions (FAQs)	How to start a picture collection (not whole films) and tag them individually? How to build a "database"	15
	Technical Support	Has classification format changed?	17
Chat	Chat	Links for Identification and Further Reading	13
	Elephant Discussion Board	Elephants and insects	14
	Ask Us Anything-2nd Chimp&See Anniversary Board-April 25th, 2017	Thank You!!!	15
Science	Questions for the Science Team	A civet is not a cat??	12
	Chimp&See General Discussion	New hashtagging guidelines for number of chimps-please read carefully :-)	14
	The Objects	Hunting discussion - Man with gun carries dead Diana Monkey	17

Table 3. Codes used to label discussion posts

Code	Description
Data collection	Activities considered within this code include: Volunteering to perform CS tasks, sharing availability, discussion of data collection methodologies, sharing data sources and personal/best practices to follow, sending reminders, and making announcements
Data analysis	Activities considered within this code include: expressing doubts and concerns related to data analysis and requesting others' opinions about the doubts expressed
Giving help	Activities considered within this code include: offering help in the form of additional resources, e.g., web pages, recommendations, tutorials, or as written instructions or as comments, asking further details about technical problems reported by volunteers, and proposing workarounds to solve technical problem
Request help	Activities considered within this code include: Asking questions in the form of what?, what do you think?, do you know?, how?, why? etc., describing problems, requesting clarifications or more information, and making technical requests
Discussion	Activities considered within this code include: encouraging discussion, providing arguments and opinions, agree/disagree on new ideas/suggestions
Updates	Activities considered within this code include: updates related to volunteer's tasks and introduction to new members who are joining the project, e.g., moderators.
Initiating	Activities considered within this code include: Proposals of new ideas/ suggestions and requesting others opinions regarding those new ideas.
Organising activities	Activities considered within this code include: details about specific events that are being organized within the context of the project e.g., year-end activities, gift distributions etc. or events planned for the future, organising how to distribute tasks, and invitations for collaboration.
Sharing knowledge	Activities considered within this code include: sharing knowledge from a previous or from a current CS project, lessons learned, sharing experiences, and providing reasoning to support an argument or an action taken

Modelling Discourse Using ENA. ENA webtool[4] was used to model the discourse. In ENA, a network model is generated for a given unit of analysis considering the co-occurrences of the codes within a defined conversation. Conversations include lines of data from which we identify or "dig" connections for a given unit of analysis. Links can only be established within a defined conversation.

The three user roles, i.e., volunteers, moderators, and scientists were set as our units of analysis. The conversations were defined by the types of discussion boards. We chose the moving stanza window method to model discussions. Using this method, the discourse elements (codes) are segmented according to their temporal proximity. The size of the window determines the co-occurrences that are considered and thus limits the possible connections [22]. We selected a moving stanza window size of 4. A window of size 2 would lead to a Markov type

---

[4] Epistemic Network Analysis, Wisconsin Center for Education Research: https://www.epistemicnetwork.org. Retrieved: 2021-04-26.

model with only one-step dependencies. The size of the moving stanza window was chosen after a qualitative assessment of the posts to capture meaningful connections in discourse [22].

3   Analysis Results

3.1   Social Networks and Role Dynamics

The sociogram of the extracted network is shown in Fig. 1. To highlight a relevant portion of the network, 10-core filtering has been applied. Except a single volunteer, the densely connected component shows mainly moderators and scientists that have a high outdegree.

Following the conceptualisation of social capital mentioned before, this might indicate the feeling of importance to communicate with people of higher reputation. Therefore, we investigate the direction of communication, in particularly, who references whom in terms of affiliated forum role. The following analysis considers the whole communication structure and is not restricted to the superusers.

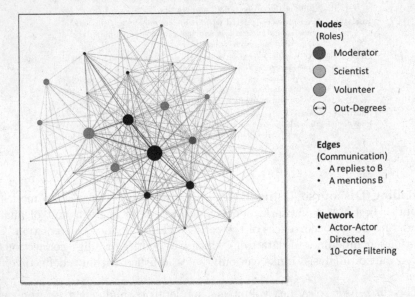

Fig. 1. The extracted sociogram of all boards over all time slices shows the relative importance of moderators in contrast to volunteers. Node labels have been hidden due to privacy reasons.

Figure 2 shows the relative amount of references, normalized by the total number of references over all user roles in the specific forum. A reference is either a direct mentioning of a user (with the '@' symbol) or a post reply in the conversation structure of the discussion forum. In the help forum, most references are

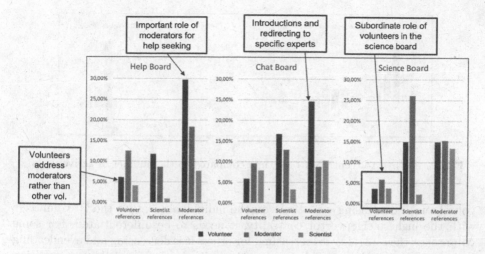

Fig. 2. Who talks to whom? Distribution of messages grouped by source role and board.

made by moderators. When volunteers seek for help, they typically do not know whom to address, whereas moderators might point to scientists and/or mention the user who asked a question. The investigation of epistemic aspects in Sect. 2.2 is dedicated to this. Volunteers typically reference moderators to say "thanks" regarding the prior reply to the help seeking. In the chat board, the references are similar, except that there is less need for moderators to direct to scientists, which explains the lower bar for this reference. Volunteers are mentioned quite often in this forum, usually because the moderators and scientists welcome them. The chat forum is sometimes used by users to introduce themselves. This can serve for further analyses to deepen the understanding of the incentives and backgrounds of volunteers, and particularly their motivation to participate in CS activities. Interestingly, the figures indicate that scientists mostly communicate with persons from other roles, not with other scientists. Such patterns are reasonable under the premise that the communication is well-coordinated, for example, when help seeking is directed towards scientists by moderators, who know their levels of expertise. Particularly in professional contexts, such a knowledge awareness is quite important for successful teamwork. Overall, these distributions of forum communication reveal that particularly moderators play an important role in the mediation of citizen science activities. On the opposite, volunteers play a subordinate role particularly in the content-related forum, the science board.

The feeling to communicate with people of higher reputation is backed by the change of eigenvector centrality over time. For all roles, we could observe a drop in active users over time, the most drastic on the part of the volunteers (cf. Fig. 3). Although, this implies that the change in eigenvector centrality is caused by the drop of users and just an anomaly of the data, the tracing of the change over time on the individual level is twofold: While the average for some

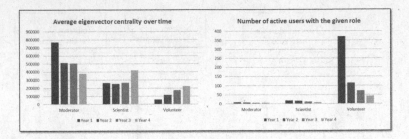

Fig. 3. Eigenvector centrality over time compared to the number of active users.

volunteers is decreasing over time, on the individual level for the 10 volunteers with the highest eigenvector centrality, it needs to be differentiated. For some volunteers, the centrality is increasing, for others it is decreasing and even leading to a drop out (cf. Fig. 4). This seems to be in line with the previous assumption that volunteers are aspiring to enter a network of higher reputation and thus boost their own influence, or when they can not enter such a network decrease and/or drop out. On the part of the moderators, a decrease in centrality could be observed on the individual level for most of the 8 moderators. In the two cases without a decrease, the moderators stopped posting and thus dropped out. For the scientists, we could not observe any comparable patterns.

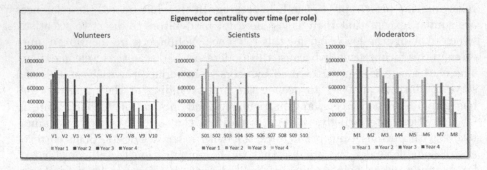

Fig. 4. Eigenvector centrality over time for the highest ranking actors.

3.2   Epistemic Networks and Discourse Structures

Epistemic Networks (EN) generated for different user roles considering different discussion boards are shown in Fig. 5. As shown in Fig. 5, in the Help Board volunteers and moderators exhibit similar behaviours as they often made connections among help-seeking and help-giving (strong connections between *Request Help* and *Giving Help* codes are visible). Notably, the EN of scientists in the Help Board does not exhibit connections to *Request Help* code rather strong connections between *Giving Help*, *Discussion*, *Sharing Knowledge*, and *Updates* are visible. This indicates that the scientists act as knowledge providers who bring knowledge from previous CS projects, sharing relevant experiences and lessons learned (see Table 3 description for *Sharing Knowledge* code). Moreover, connections to the code *Updates* indicate that in these discussion spaces scientists contribute with important updates that are necessary to carry out the intended CS task.

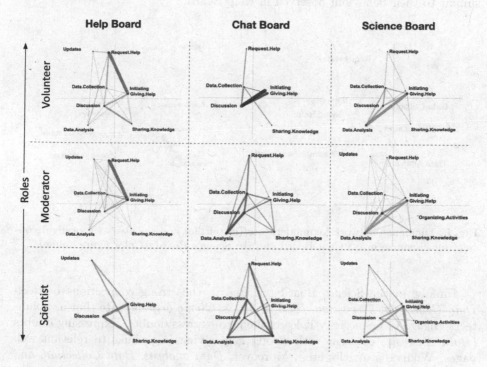

Fig. 5. Discourse patterns by user groups considering three boards.

When considering the Chat Board (cf. Fig. 5) the strong connections observed for volunteers (e.g., between *Discussion*, *Giving Help* and *Initiating* codes) can be interpreted as discussions in terms of providing opinions and (dis)agreeing with others opinions lead to proposal of new ideas (code: *Initiating*). Similarly, giving help (e.g., sharing links to related web pages, tutorials, etc.) also leads to discussion and initiation of new ideas in the chat board. As it can be seen in Fig. 5 the networks generated for moderators and scientists for Chat and Science Boards show a similar network structure. Difference networks were generated to disentangle the differences in discourse between moderators and the scientists in Chat and Science Boards (cf. Fig. 6).

As shown in Fig. 6(a) the strong connections between *Data Analysis* and *Discussion* for moderators in the Chat Board indicate that as they engage in data analysis they share doubts or concerns and engaged in discussion to solve those. The connection between *Data Collection*, *Giving help* and *Discussion* indicate that as they engage in data collection, e.g., sharing observations, tagging etc. they often request others opinions and sometimes offer help all the while moderating discussion. As shown in the difference network (see Fig. 6(a)) in the Chat-Board a number of connections to *Sharing Knowledge* indicate that scientists engage in sharing knowledge regarding various aspects. This behaviour is similar to their behaviour observed in Help Board.

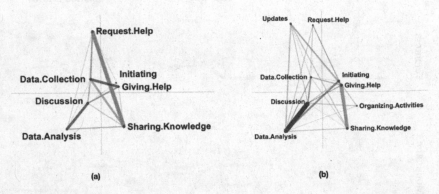

(a)   (b)

Fig. 6. Difference network for moderators (in purple) and scientists (in orange) considering discourse in (a) Chat Board and (b) Science Board. (Color figure online)

Finally, in the Science Board (cf. Fig. 5), the strong connections between *Data Collection*, *Discussion*, *Data Analysis*, *Giving help* indicate that as volunteers engage in CS activity it leads them to express doubts. Expressing doubts (*Data Analysis*) co-occur with strong help giving (e.g., links to relevant web pages, Wikipedia articles etc.). Moreover, *Data analysis*, *Data Collection*, and *Giving Help* are connected with *Discussion* showing that sharing doubts, sharing observations, and sharing additional resources lead to collective discussion.

Regarding moderators, a strong connection between *Data Analysis* and *Discussion* (cf. Fig. 6(b)) shows that in the Science Board moderators expressed doubts or concerns regarding *Data Collection* and engaged in the *Discussion* to solve those doubts. Similar connections in the EN diagrams are observed for moderators in the chat board as well. The scientists seem to share their own experiences, previous knowledge as well as directions to additional resources (connections between *Sharing Knowledge* and *Giving Help* codes) (cf. Fig. 6(b)). Moreover, connections between *Giving Help*, *Updates*, and *Data Analysis* in Fig. 6(b) indicate that in situations where additional knowledge or resources shared can not solve doubts and concerns related to CS task, scientists discussed those doubts with other scientists and attempted to facilitate the activity. The following excerpt indicate such connections.

Moderator: *I am still a bit unhappy about the vocal tags, because I am still missing the case: there is an animal seen (maybe even a chimp or baboon), but* *the vocalisation is off camera (by same species). I would like to make that clearer, as both tags - for me - do not transport that message. Especially with the baboons, but sometimes also with chimps, the individuals are reacting to that vocalization not seen and that's interesting.*

Scientist: *Hi @anonymous(name of moderator removed) - as far as I can remember, I've only used #0_chimponce. I discussed the matter with @anonymous(name of scientist removed) afterwards and subsequently removed the tag. You must have come across my post within this short time window. I am sorry for any confusion this may have caused!*

4 Discussion

The results obtained using SNA and ENA revealed interesting findings about participation and collaboration patterns of different stakeholder groups in a CS online community that could not be obtained using either of the techniques alone. ENA results indicated that in general volunteers and moderators engaged in help-seeking and help-giving in the Help Board. However, SNA further indicated that in many instances volunteers were unaware to whom the help requests need to be addressed. In certain situations when moderators lacked the knowledge to handle such help requests they were seen to notify and obtain help from the science team. These findings are aligned with findings from previous similar research [19,24].

Moreover, ENA indicated that in the Chat and Science Boards volunteers and moderators not only engaged in assigned CS task, e.g., tagging, classification (coded under *Data Collection*) within the duration of the project, rather they also engage in sharing opinions, doubts and concerns which seems to lead the initiation of new ideas that often matches with their own interests. These types of initiations are referred to as the *citizen led inquiries* [24] that opens new pathways for knowledge production and eventually leads to citizen initiated discoveries [19]. Initiation was not seen to co-occur frequently in the case of scientists indicating that the knowledge they shared is in a different format as also shown in previous research [19].

The findings of the SNA also confirmed the important role moderators play in the Chat Board mediating CS activities in these discussion spaces. Findings of SNA also indicated that in Chat Board volunteers were referred more often by scientists and moderators to welcome and introduce them in the discussion forum. The analysis of the centralities of the different actors has shown that volunteers seem to aspire establishing a network of higher reputation. Being connected to prestigious people, either scientists or moderators, might be an important key to understand motivational factors for volunteers participating in citizen science activities. The nature of Zooniverse projects foresees different models to recruit moderators, particularly from the volunteers. Unfortunately, the data has been extracted ex-post and thus we could not answer the question based on evidence, whether some volunteers have been casted to moderators. Future qualitative studies might investigate those aspects further.

When considering the role of scientists ENA indicated that it is common for the scientists to intervene in talk pages in all three boards to share knowledge.

The findings of the study need to be interpreted with caution given the limited number of talk pages selected to generate EN. It is known that CS projects are unique not only based on its participants, methodology, goals, design, etc. but also in terms of generated data and knowledge production [17, 19]. Hence in the future it is important to automate the manual coding process and to extend our analysis considering more than one CS project to produce generalizable study findings.

5   Conclusions and Future Work

Understanding the dynamics in discussion spaces of CS projects is important not only to characterise and distinguish different forms of participation and expertise of different user groups, but it also opens the prospect of improving the practice of CS in a wide variety of application fields. These include formal educational contexts as well as strategic support for policy makers [11, 19].

As a caveat, we have to consider that the analysed data and obtained results are based on forum discussions. However, such crowd-sourced citizen science activities have their focus in the collection of data and classification of objects by volunteers. The active participation in forum discussions only captures a small portion of the users activities, not directly including the collection and classification of source data. Due to limited access to the Zooniverse platform, we do not have any insights in the active participation beyond the forum activity. Future studies might take this into account, particularly to assess to what extent communication and knowledge building are interdependent with the active participation in the core of the citizen science activities.

Acknowledgements. This work was partially funded by the European Union in the context of the CS Track (Grant Agreement no. 872522) under the Horizon 2020 program. This document does not represent the opinion of the European Union, and the European Union is not responsible for any use that might be made of its content. We thank all CS Track team members for the fruitful interactions that facilitated this work.

References

1. Aristeidou, M., Scanlon, E., Sharples, M.: Profiles of engagement in online communities of citizen science participation. Comput. Hum. Behav. **74**, 246–256 (2017)
2. Bastian, M., Heymann, S., Jacomy, M.: Gephi: an open source software for exploring and manipulating networks (2009)
3. Bonacich, P.: Power and centrality: a family of measures. Am. J. Sociol. **92**(5), 1170–1182 (1987)
4. Bonney, R., et al.: Public participation in scientific research: defining the field and assessing its potential for informal science education. A CAISE Inquiry Group report. ERIC (2009). Online Submission

5. Borgatti, S.P., Mehra, A., Brass, D.J., Labianca, G.: Network analysis in the social sciences. Science **323**(5916), 892–895 (2009)
6. Brin, S., Page, L.: The anatomy of a large-scale hypertextual web search engine. Comput. Netw. ISDN Syst. **30**(1–7), 107–117 (1998)
7. Chang, H.H., Chuang, S.S.: Social capital and individual motivations on knowledge sharing: participant involvement as a moderator. Inf. Manag. **48**(1), 9–18 (2011)
8. Csanadi, A., Eagan, B., Kollar, I., Shaffer, D.W., Fischer, F.: When coding-and-counting is not enough: using epistemic network analysis (ENA) to analyze verbal data in CSCL research. Int. J. Comput.-Support. Collab. Learn. **13**(4), 419–438 (2018). https://doi.org/10.1007/s11412-018-9292-z
9. Glaser, B.G., Strauss, A.L.: The Discovery of Grounded Theory: Strategies for Qualitative Research. Aldine Transaction, New Brunswick (1967)
10. Haklay, M.M., Dörler, D., Heigl, F., Manzoni, M., Hecker, S., Vohland, K.: What is citizen science? The challenges of definition. In: Vohland, K., et al. (eds.) The Science of Citizen Science, pp. 13–33. Springer, Cham (2021). https://doi.org/10.1007/978-3-030-58278-4_2
11. Haklay, M.: Citizen science and policy: a European perspective. Woodrow Wilson International Center for Scholars, Washington, DC (2015)
12. Hollenbeck, J.R., Jamieson, B.B.: Human capital, social capital, and social network analysis: implications for strategic human resource management. Acad. Manag. Perspect. **29**(3), 370–385 (2015)
13. Hoppe, H.U., Harrer, A., Göhnert, T., Hecking, T.: Applying network models and network analysis techniques to the study of online communities. In: Cress, U., Moskaliuk, J., Jeong, H. (eds.) Mass Collaboration and Education. CCLS, vol. 16, pp. 347–366. Springer, Cham (2016). https://doi.org/10.1007/978-3-319-13536-6_17
14. Huang, J., et al.: Scientific discourse of citizen scientists: models as a boundary object for collaborative problem solving. Comput. Hum. Behav. **87**, 480–492 (2018)
15. Kullenberg, C., Kasperowski, D.: What is citizen science? A scientometric meta-analysis. PLoS ONE **11**(1), e0147152 (2016)
16. Lave, J., Wenger, E.: Legitimate peripheral participation. Learners, learning and assessment. The Open University, London (2016)
17. Lemmens, R., et al.: A conceptual model for participants and activities in citizen science projects. In: Vohland, K., et al. (eds.) The Science of Citizen Science, pp. 159–182. Springer, Cham (2021). https://doi.org/10.1007/978-3-030-58278-4_9
18. Newman, G., Wiggins, A., Crall, A., Graham, E., Newman, S., Crowston, K.: The future of citizen science: emerging technologies and shifting paradigms. Front. Ecol. Environ. **10**(6), 298–304 (2012)
19. Rohden, F., Kullenberg, C., Hagen, N., Kasperowski, D.: Tagging, pinging and linking-user roles in virtual citizen science forums. Citiz. Sci. Theory Pract. **4**(1), 19 (2019)
20. Shaffer, D.W., Collier, W., Ruis, A.R.: A tutorial on epistemic network analysis: analyzing the structure of connections in cognitive, social, and interaction data. J. Learn. Anal. **3**(3), 9–45 (2016)
21. Buckingham Shum, S., Echeverria, V., Martinez-Maldonado, R.: The multimodal matrix as a quantitative ethnography methodology. In: Eagan, B., Misfeldt, M., Siebert-Evenstone, A. (eds.) ICQE 2019. CCIS, vol. 1112, pp. 26–40. Springer, Cham (2019). https://doi.org/10.1007/978-3-030-33232-7_3
22. Siebert-Evenstone, A.L., Irgens, G.A., Collier, W., Swiecki, Z., Ruis, A.R., Shaffer, D.W.: In search of conversational grain size: modelling semantic structure using moving stanza windows. J. Learn. Anal. **4**(3), 123–139 (2017)

23. Simpson, R., Page, K.R., De Roure, D.: Zooniverse: observing the world's largest citizen science platform (2014)
24. Tinati, R., Van Kleek, M., Simperl, E., Luczak-Rösch, M., Simpson, R., Shadbolt, N.: Designing for citizen data analysis: a cross-sectional case study of a multi-domain citizen science platform. ACM (2015)
25. Wasserman, S., Faust, K.: Social Network Analysis: Methods and Applications. Cambridge University Press, Cambridge (1999)

Work-in-Progress Papers

Homogeneous Student Engagement: A Strategy for Group Formation During Online Learning

Victoria Abou-Khalil$^{(\boxtimes)}$ ⓘ and Hiroaki Ogata ⓘ

Academic Center for Computing and Media Studies, Kyoto University, Kyoto, Japan

Abstract. Group discussions can be beneficial to keep students engaged during online learning provided that group members form a good match. For instance, the success of the group depends to a great extent on the engagement of its group members. During the COVID-19 pandemic, it became possible to automatically detect engagement using students learning data as all the teaching and learning processes can be recorded. This paper presents an exploratory study that compares the grouping of students with homogeneous engagement levels together to the grouping of students with heterogeneous engagement levels together. We measured the student engagement using their activity logs in an e-book system. We conducted a study with 23 students enrolled in an online class and analyzed the impact of different grouping styles on the learning achievement and student satisfaction of low, mid, and high engagement students. The results show that grouping students with homogeneous engagement levels together is associated with a significant increase in the learning achievement of low-engagement students and the satisfaction of high-engagement students.

Keywords: Group formation · Student engagement · Emergency remote teaching · Online learning

1 Introduction

The increase in emergency remote teaching during the COVID-19 pandemic raised concerns about a decrease in student engagement. The online classes resulted in a decrease in typical interactions that students experience in a classroom like the student-student interaction [2,3,11]. Studies conducted during the COVID-19 pandemic reported low student engagement during group activities [1]. This might be due to teachers grouping students randomly as they are mostly anonymous to them [16]. Even though these issues were highlighted during the pandemic, they remain applicable for synchronous online classes.

Choosing an effective criterion for group formation during online classes can be a challenging, yet critical step. Group formation is essential in designing collaborative learning activities as the success of the group depends to a great extent on the matching of the group members [8]. Group formation during online classes

© Springer Nature Switzerland AG 2021
D. Hernández-Leo et al. (Eds.): CollabTech 2021, LNCS 12856, pp. 85–92, 2021.
https://doi.org/10.1007/978-3-030-85071-5_6

is challenging due to a difficulty connecting with fellow students [12] technical problems, occasional absence of camera, and lack of out-of-class student-student interactions. Moreover, in a online groupwork, and with limited instructor supervision, some students might limit their participation. Such learners with limited or low engagement might affect the groupwork [14]. Thus, it is important to take into consideration the engagement level of students when forming groups in a synchronous online learning environment. The most important forms of interaction to keep students engaged during remote learning is student-content interaction. Student-content interaction refers to students' interaction with the content that results in a change in their understanding, perspective, or cognitive structure [11]. Through student-content interactions, learners construct meaning, relate the content to previous knowledge, and apply it to problem-solving [5]. It became possible to automatically detect engagement using students learning data in an online learning environment as all the teaching and learning processes can be recorded [13].

In this work, we propose to group students based on their student-content engagement, measured using their activity logs in an e-book system. We compare the learning achievement and satisfaction when grouping students by with similar engagement levels together versus grouping students with different engagement levels together. The research questions guiding the study were: 1. How does grouping students based on student-content engagement levels affect the learning achievement during online classes? 2. How does grouping students based on student-content engagement levels affect the satisfaction levels during online classes? 3. How are the learning achievements and satisfaction of low, mid, and high- engagement students affected by homogeneous groups and heterogeneous formation groups?

In the following sections, we first present the criteria used for group formation. Then, we present the experiment setup and execution in an online classroom. Finally, we show the experiment results and present our conclusions and future work.

2   Methods

2.1   Experiment Design

Participants. Participants were 23 graduate students of a graduate college in Japan. All students were enrolled in the same class where the experiment took place. The class was a design thinking class that was delivered synchronously online due to restrictions resulting from the COVID-19 pandemic. The students only met each other online and experienced regular group work activities. The medium of instruction was English.

Procedure. We conducted a study that involves two pre/post tests measures of learning achievement and satisfaction after different group formations. The study was conducted over two phases of two weeks each and is shown in Fig. 1.

At the beginning of every week of each phase, the instructor gave the students an individual homework that consisted of 1) reading a document about a specific topic using an e-book reader 2) pre-test that consists of answering a set of questions on the topic. During week 2 of every phase, the instructor divided the students into groups based on their online engagement with the document and asked them to critically discuss the document. After the discussion ended, students took a post-test that evaluates student understanding of the topic as well a questionnaire that measures their satisfaction with the groupwork. The instructor grouped together students with different engagement levels in phase 1 and students with similar levels in phase 2.

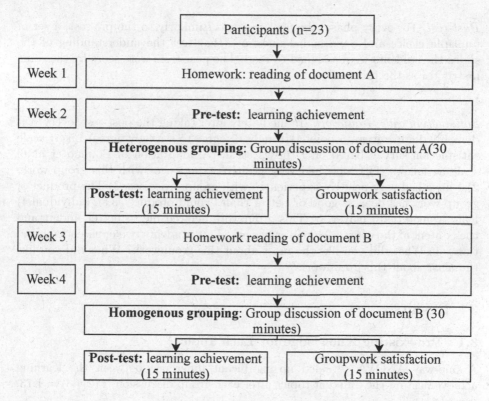

Fig. 1. Experimental procedure

Measurements

Engagement. We used the e-book interaction logs to measure student engagement. Trace data such as timestamps, notes, or learning material accessed strongly supports inferences about students' cognition and satisfaction and has been used as a proxy for student engagement [10,17]. At the beginning of each phase, we gave the students a homework that consisted of slides to read on the e-book reader and measured student engagement by looking at three variables:

1) Completion rate i.e. percentages of slides read, 2) time spent reading the slides, and 3) number of markers and memos added to the reading material. The three variables were given equal weight and transformed into percentile ranks. Based on the final score and the percentile rank, the students were categorized into eight low, six mid, and nine high engagement.

Pre-test. For every phase, the pre-test was composed of multiple choice questions and open ended questions testing the understanding of the slides the student were assigned to read. The pre-tests were scored by the instructor.

Post-test. For every phase, the post-test was, similarly to the pre-test, a set of multiple choice and open ended questions that test the understanding of the slides the students were assigned to read. The post-tests were score by the same instructor as the pre-test.

Satisfaction with Groupwork. Immediately after taking the post-test, every student filled a five-item, 5 point (strongly disagree to strongly agree) Likert scale satisfaction survey based on Drudy's et al. [7] adaptation of Bonnao et al.[6] scale as follows: 1) I have had very positive experiences with this group work. 2) I have had very positive experiences with group processes. 3) The product of group work has been as good or better than I could produce as an individual.4) I am a good team player. 5) This groupwork allowed me to better understand the content of the course. Moreover, we asked the students two open-ended questions. 1) What did you like the most about this groupwork? What did you like the least about this groupwork?

3   Results

3.1   Pre-existing Knowledge for Each Topic

A one-way ANOVA revealed no significant difference between the learning achievement on the different topics after each group discussion, $F(2, 66) = 1.73$, $p = .18$.

3.2   Learning Achievement and Satisfaction

We used a t-test to analyze the differences in learning achievement and satisfaction after grouping students by homogeneous engagement levels and grouping them by heterogeneous engagement levels. The results show no significance difference in the learning achievements and satisfaction of students following the two different grouping types $t(23) = 0.37$, $p = 0.71$; $t(23) = 0.26$, $p = 0.79$, respectively.

To deepen the analysis, the scores of low, mid and high engagement students were analyzed separately as shown in Table 1. Low engagement students perform significantly better after a discussion with students with similar engagement levels. There is no significant difference in the learning achievements of mid and high engagement students when they are grouped with student with similar engagement levels and with students with different engagement levels.

Table 1. Learning achievement of low, mid, and high engagement students in homogeneous and heterogeneous group work

	Low engagement				Mid engagement				High engagement			
	Mean	SD	t	d	Mean	SD	t	d	Mean	SD	t	d
Homog	6.50	2.27	2.22[a]	1.11	5.17	0.75	0.11	0.06	6.78	2.11	1.28	0.60
Heterog	3.75	2.66			5.00	3.41			5.33	2.65		

[a] $<.05$

A t-test was used to analyze the differences in the satisfaction of students with their group work when they are grouped by homogeneous engagement levels or by heterogeneous engagement levels. The answers of low, mid and high engagement students were analyzed separately as shown in Table 2. The results show that the satisfaction of high engagement students is significantly higher when they are grouped with students with similar engagement levels.

Table 2. Satisfaction of low, mid, and high engagement students in homogeneous and heterogeneous group work

	Low engagement				Mid engagement				High engagement			
	Mean	SD	t	d	Mean	SD	t	d	Mean	SD	t	d
Homog.	3.87	0.58	0.13	0.06	3.25	1.54	1.19	0.64	4.12	0.91	0.78[a]	0.39
Heterog.	3.82	0.51			4.00	0.60			3.78	0.79		

[a] $<.05$

3.3 Student Experience

We analyzed the responses to the open-ended questions using a quantitative content analysis method [4,9]. We chose "what students liked the most", "what students liked the least" as a sampling unit and coded the answers to the open-ended question. The results are shown in Tables 3 and 4.

Table 3. What students liked the most about the groupwork

	Homogeneous grouping (%)	Heterogeneous grouping (%)
Active participation of all group members	66.6	22.7
Better understanding of content	16.6	45.4
Mutual support	0.0	18.1
Meeting new people	8.3	0.0
Having fun	8.3	4.5
Learning new thinking methods	0.0	4.5

Table 4. What students liked the least about the groupwork

	Homogeneous grouping (%)	Heterogeneous grouping (%)
Some participants are inactive	30.7	57.1
Conversation about private matters	30.7	7.1
Non-focused discussion	0.0	28.5
Negative thoughts	23.0	0.0
Limited understanding of the topic	15.3	0.0
One person is taking over	0.0	7.1

4   Discussion

We conducted a preliminary study to compare the grouping of students with homogeneous and heterogeneous engagement levels during online learning. The results show that using homogeneous student engagement as a group formation criteria can increase the learning achievement of low-engagement students and the satisfaction of high-engagement students. This could be the result of a higher student participation as reported by the participants through the open questions.

Our results are in line with the work of Sanz-Martinez and colleagues that showed that groups formed based on homogeneous student engagement during MOOCs had higher rates of task-completion and peer interactions. Moreover, similarly to our study, students reported higher levels of satisfaction compared to students in more heterogeneous groups [14,15]. The results showing an increase in learning achievement of the low engagement students are in line with Wichmann et al.'s study that showed that low-level students were more productive in homogeneous groups, suggesting that grouping less active students together, makes social loafing more difficult and students participate more [18]. With the absence of students with better knowledge of the material within the group, low engagement students cannot count on the students who already know the material and have more pressure to understand it themselves.

Even though the results were extracted during the online classes provided during the COVID-19 pandemic, their applicability to face to face group activities could be investigated.

The biggest limitation of this study is the small number of participants. This is acceptable in the context of a preliminary investigation. Future studies that aim to confirm our results would require a larger number of participants.

5   Conclusion

In this paper, we have presented the results of a preliminary study that compares the grouping of students with homogeneous engagement levels together to the grouping of students with heterogeneous engagement levels during online classes. We show that grouping students with similar engagement levels together significantly increases the learning achievement of low engagement students and the satisfaction of high engagement students.

References

1. Abou-Khalil, V., Helou, S., Khalifé, E., Chen, M.A., Majumdar, R., Ogata, H.: Emergency online learning in low-resource settings: effective student engagement strategies. Educ. Sci. **11**(1), 24 (2021). Publisher: Multidisciplinary Digital Publishing Institute
2. Abou-Khalil, V., Helou, S., Khalifé, E., Majumdar, R., Ogata, H.: Emergency remote teaching in low-resource contexts: how did teachers adapt? In: Proceedings of the 28th International Conference on Computers in Education, vol. I, pp. 686–688, November 2020
3. Anderson, T., Garrison, D.R.: Learning in a networked world: new roles and responsibilties. In: Distance Learners in Higher Education: Institutional Responses for Quality Outcomes. Atwood, Madison (1998)
4. Berelson, B.: Content analysis in communication research (1952). Publisher: Free press
5. Bernard, R.M., et al.: A meta-analysis of three types of interaction treatments in distance education. Rev. Educ. Res. **79**(3), 1243–1289 (2009). Publisher: Sage Publications
6. Bonanno, H., Jones, J., English, L.: Improving group satisfaction: making groups work in a first-year undergraduate course. Teach. High. Educ. **3**(3), 365–382 (1998). Publisher: Taylor & Francis
7. Drury, H., Kay, J., Losberg, W.: Student satisfaction with groupwork in undergraduate computer science: do things get better? In: Proceedings of the Fifth Australasian Conference on Computing Education, vol. 20, pp. 77–85 (2003)
8. Isotani, S., Inaba, A., Ikeda, M., Mizoguchi, R.: An ontology engineering approach to the realization of theory-driven group formation. Int. J. Comput. Support. Collab. Learn. **4**(4), 445–478 (2009). Publisher: Springer
9. Krippendorff, K.: Content Analysis: An Introduction to Its Methodology. Sage publications, California (2018)
10. Lin, C.C., Tsai, C.C.: Participatory learning through behavioral and cognitive engagements in an online collective information searching activity. Int. J. Comput. Support. Collab. Learn. **7**(4), 543–566 (2012). Publisher: Springer
11. Moore, M.G.: Three Types of Interaction. Taylor & Francis, London (1989)
12. Naughton, C.L.: Effects of synchronous group work on learning and community in online mathematics at community colleges (2020)
13. Ogata, H., et al.: E-Book-based learning analytics in university education. In: International Conference on Computer in Education (ICCE 2015), pp. 401–406 (2015)
14. Sanz-Martínez, L., Er, E., Martínez-Monés, A., Dimitriadis, Y., Bote-Lorenzo, M.L.: Creating collaborative groups in a MOOC: a homogeneous engagement grouping approach. Behav. Inf. Technol. **38**(11), 1107–1121 (2019). Publisher: Taylor & Francis

15. Sanz-Martínez, L., Martínez-Monés, A., Bote-Lorenzo, M.L., Muñoz-Cristóbal, J.A., Dimitriadis, Y.: Automatic group formation in a MOOC based on students' activity criteria. In: Lavoué, É., Drachsler, H., Verbert, K., Broisin, J., Pérez-Sanagustín, M. (eds.) EC-TEL 2017. LNCS, vol. 10474, pp. 179–193. Springer, Cham (2017). https://doi.org/10.1007/978-3-319-66610-5_14
16. Sharma, P., Maleyeff, J.: Internet education: potential problems and solutions. Int. J. Educ. Manag. **17**, 19–25 (2003). Publisher: MCB UP Ltd
17. Vytasek, J.M., Patzak, A., Winne, P.H.: Analytics for student engagement. In: Machine Learning Paradigms, pp. 23–48. Springer (2020)
18. Wichmann, A., Hecking, T., Elson, M., Christmann, N., Herrmann, T., Hoppe, H.U.: Group formation for small-group learning: are heterogeneous groups more productive? In: Proceedings of the 12th International Symposium on Open Collaboration, pp. 1–4 (2016)

Supporting Peer Evaluation in a Data-Driven Group Learning Environment

Liang Changhao[✉] [iD], Yuko Toyokawa, Taro Nakanishi, Rwitajit Majumdar[iD], and Hiroaki Ogata[iD]

Kyoto University, Kyoto 606-8501, Japan
liang.changhao.84c@st.kyoto-u.ac.jp

Abstract. In collaborative learning, peer evaluation plays a substantial role during group work implementation. To scaffold learners to peer evaluate, the design of a digital supportive system is presented in this paper. The system enables students to evaluate peers within their own group as well as other groups' output with the real-time visualization of feedback from peers. The peer evaluation function is studied in a demonstration experiment at a high school context. It is found that the groups worked actively to conduct peer evaluation using the system. Future possibilities are discussed about how to use the Group Learning Orchestration Based on Evidence (GLOBE) framework to consider the evaluation score as another feature for subsequent grouping in the system.

Keywords: Collaborative learning · Group evaluation · Peer evaluation · Learning analytics · CSCL

1 Introduction

Collaborative skill, one of the critical soft skills in today's society, is becoming increasingly demanded [7]. In the wake of the trend of the flipped classroom and self-regulated learning which calls for more subjectivity, computer-supported collaborative learning (CSCL) provides a powerful solution conducting group work in a data-driven learning analytics environment [10].

In the existing group work practice, problems of social loafing and free riding [18] are prevalent and only the teacher's evaluation is not enough since one teacher cannot identify the performance of each student in the class [11], especially in the online environment. Therefore, peer evaluation is required to alleviate teachers' workload and provide an overall inspection across the group work process. In this paper, we present a peer evaluation system linked to learning analytics infrastructure and its classroom implementation. Teachers and learners can provide an evaluation by rating and commenting and get real-time feedback as well. Meanwhile, these assessment data will be logged and cyclically used in the other stages of the data-driven group work support circulate.

A part of this paper was supported by JSPS KAKENHI 16H06304 and 20K20131 and NEDO JPNP20006 and JPNP18013 and SPIRITS 2020 of Kyoto University.

D. Hernández-Leo et al. (Eds.): CollabTech 2021, LNCS 12856, pp. 93–100, 2021.
https://doi.org/10.1007/978-3-030-85071-5_7

2   Related Work

Peer evaluation activity can be referred to as the process of assessing the work of peers against a various set of assessment criteria [16]. When carrying out a peer evaluation activity, teachers should set a foundation by creating effective evaluation tools, then implement formative and summative feedback during the collaborative experience, and assess the collaborative evaluation process after the activity [9].

When it comes to evaluation tools, the traditional approach uses paper-based surveys and students will tend to give a biased assessment because it is easily seen by others [19]. Later research used digital files such as PDF or computer-based survey whereas teachers still need to deal with multiple files to gather and analyze the results after the evaluation task [6]. Web pages appeared as a new solution to deal with peer evaluation online, which overcomes the accessibility problems and relieves stakeholders from complex paperwork [19]. It enhances individualism and protects the privacy of evaluators. To enrich the experience of online peer evaluation, the current work extends real-time group awareness support by using a learning analytics infrastructure.

To conduct effective evaluation activities, participants need a clear impression on how they should evaluate others, in case they will just give casual ratings or compliments thus making the evaluation invalid. Instructors should give them rubrics [2] and articulate evaluation criteria in a clear manner depending on different learning contexts, which has become a consensus in related researches [9].

Regarding the social-emotional issue, it is known that the peer evaluator is not willing to make unfavorable judgments about the person if (s)he is exposed to peers [5] because peer grading is sensitive data. Hence, to alleviate the impact of such pressure, a peer evaluation system should guarantee the privacy of evaluators and enable flexible visibility of evaluation scores depending on different contexts.

With the development of CSCL, the evaluation of group work can be delivered faster [6], thus enabling teachers to conduct the evaluation activities in a shorter time and sparing some for formative feedback. Such formative feedback is considered as a group awareness information. The group awareness information [14] refers to any information about the group that can facilitate group members to take corrective actions [13]. Participants can perform a more accurate evaluation when they have abundant information about their group members such as engagement in discussion [17].

The possibilities of re-usage of accumulated evaluation data is also seldom explored in existing system. For instance, it is proposed that those who are rejected or neglected in group work be prompted to teachers beforehand [3]. To identify those individuals, learning analytics using historical evaluation data proves to be a feasible solution. Based on evaluation data, teachers can both reflect on the variance of group work performance but also guide group formation and predict group work performance in the next activity. Despite various features mentioned above, existing system designs have limited group evaluation data aggregation and re-use capabilities.

3   System Design

The peer evaluation system proposed here works as an indispensable component of the group work support system where groups are formed using learning log data collected from any learning management system and learning behavior sensor like BookRoll (Fig. 1) [8]. The Group Work Module (GWM) in LAView [8] has two components - the group formation and the group evaluation. Peer evaluation is conducted based on the groups formed in the previous step using learning log data [4]. The peer evaluation data together with teacher's evaluation data are also logged in the learning record store and can be re-used. It also provides a data infrastructure for subsequent learning analytics research.

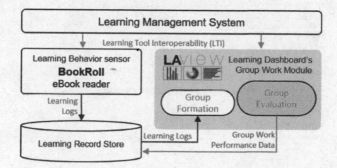

Fig. 1. Architecture of the learning analytics-enhanced group work module [12].

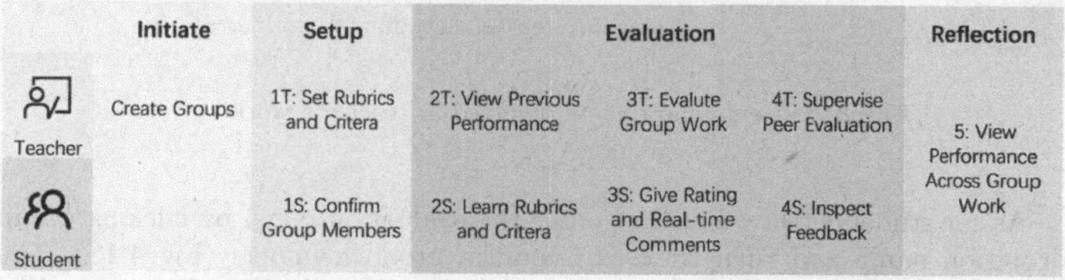

	Initiate	Setup	Evaluation				Reflection
Teacher	Create Groups	1T: Set Rubrics and Critera	2T: View Previous Performance	3T: Evalute Group Work	4T: Supervise Peer Evaluation		5: View Performance Across Group Work
Student		1S: Confirm Group Members	2S: Learn Rubrics and Critera	3S: Give Rating and Real-time Comments	4S: Inspect Feedback		

Fig. 2. Activity flow of peer evaluation using system.

Figure 2 describes the activity flow of using the system when conducting group work with a peer evaluation component. The teachers can first form groups considering the learning logs as well as previous group work performance of the students in the course [12]. Then, the peer evaluation rubrics can be configured by the teachers in the settings panel (Fig. 3-1T) either by text (Fig. 4-2Sa) or uploading a PDF (Fig. 4-2Sb) depending on different contexts. Considering the anonymity, peer evaluation scores are hidden to students default. Meanwhile, the system can automatically assign a part of groups to each student to evaluate thus lightening their workload (Fig. 4-3Sb). Before the group work, the teacher can view the previous group work performance of students illustrated by colorful emoticons (Fig. 3-2T), thus figuring out those with a higher tendency to low performance. During the peer evaluation, the teacher can evaluate groups (Fig. 3-3T) and see the ratings and comments from students (Fig. 3-4T). The teacher can also inspect the distribution of the latest group work performance data to reflect on the effectiveness of any group work activity.

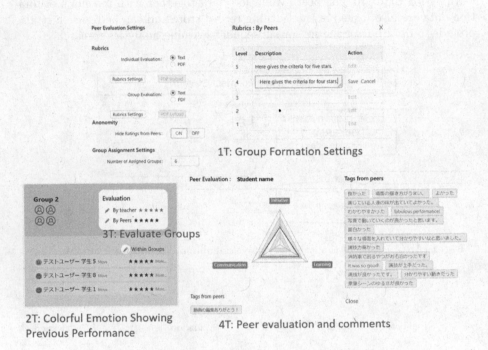

Fig. 3. System components involved in teacher's workflow.

As for students, they will first enter the evaluation panel by clicking group formation name and then they can confirm group members (Fig. 4-1S). The student should read about the rubrics provided by the teacher (Fig. 4-2S) and then evaluate in light of the criteria. During the evaluation activity, students can give rates as well as comments to supplement their opinions. The system provides them with evaluation support at both individual (Fig. 4-3Sa) and group level (Fig. 4-3Sb).

In terms of evaluation at the individual level, the student can rate in different indicators (subjectivity, communication skills, and learning) which is suggested by the Japanese Government [1]. Meanwhile, the radar denoting average group performance scores and comments from peers will be visualized promptly so that the student can respond to feedback in time (Fig. 4-4S). As for the evaluation of other groups, students can do the above-mentioned evaluations as well and the results will be integrated into the teacher's view (Fig. 4-4T).

To support the reflection stage after group work, statistical graphs provided the variation of peer scores across group work conducted in a course (Fig. 4-5). These graphs provide an overall view of the student's group learning experience.

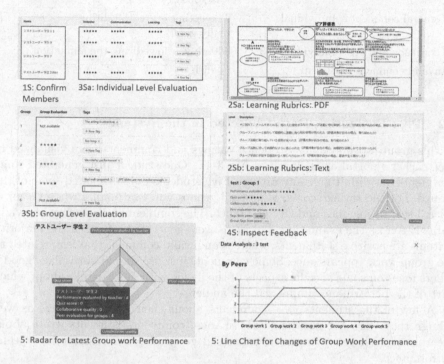

Fig. 4. System components involved in student's workflow.

4   Case Study of System Usage

4.1   Context and Activity Design

A demonstration experiment was conducted in a Grade 1 English class in high school, with 32 students working in 8 groups. Students took a pre-test on vocabulary and read an English story via online reader BookRoll [8]. Then they were heterogeneously grouped via the group formation module based on the test scores and engagement of the reading activity. Students worked in groups to make a movie in light of the story they read and then made a presentation to the whole class. After that, students were required to evaluate the performance of other groups using the system. In this practice, we used default settings with general rubrics that evaluate group work at 5 levels using stars (Fig. 4-2Sb), and each student was assigned to evaluate all other groups' presentations via rating scores and comments.

Table 1. Summary of textual comments collected in the practice.

Type	Target	Count	Examples (Translated from Japanese)
General comment	Group	82	Interesting interpretation./Ingenious!
Specific details	Group	45	The idea of using the stairs as a ladder was good
General comment	Individual	5	The acting is great!/Editing work is really good!
Gratitude and role	Individual	3	Thank you for editing the animation!
Invalid comment	Group	1	Foolish

4.2   Peer Evaluation Data Collected in the System

In this group work activity, students' ratings and comments were visualized in the teacher's portal as is shown in Fig. 3-4T. One student just generated some comments but didn't give any ratings. Five students only evaluated some of the groups. For the rating scores, almost all groups got 4 or 5 stars while Group 2 got a 3-star rating once and Group 3 twice. The comments collected are shown in Table 1. Across the evaluation, 128 items were generated, of which the majority of items are positive statements, whereas an invalid comment that is unrelated to the group work appears once. Some comments just use simple words like "good", others focus on some specific aspects of the movie with more details about which part of the performance impressed the audience.

A few of the students gave comments about their group members as well though they were not instructed to. In these comments, students wrote about the role of each group member, expressed gratitude, and remarked on peers' performance.

4.3   Initial User Feedback to the System

A preliminary usability survey was conducted after the group work. Students mentioned that the system enabled them to exchange ideas efficiently using comments in an anonymous context. They also said it was easy to know group members and get visualized performance data, which agreed with the impact of group awareness information [17]. On the other hand, some students mentioned the complexity of learning and the obscurity of default rubrics, which should be improved in the next experiment. Besides, we also received informal feedback from teachers who stressed the care for the sensitivity of evaluation data of students, which follows the anonymity issue [5].

5   Discussion and Future Work

In this paper, we introduced components of a peer evaluation system in the data-driven group learning environment and its activity workflow. Compared with existing evaluation approaches mentioned in Sect. 2, the system not only serves as a simple tool for conducting peer evaluation at both individual and group levels but also visualizes previous performance for teachers as an indication and provides group awareness information to the group members. From the classroom implementation study, we confirmed that the system helps students to do peer evaluation efficiently in an actual class.

However, the empirical study in this paper is limited to a single context of high school English class. More group activities in different contexts are required to collect enough data for any comparative study. Meanwhile, the impact of evaluation data on group formation and other stages deserves further exploration. At present, we could not provide enough group awareness information [17] due to the limitation of engagement data since we have not connected the forum data nor voice data to the present system. Group awareness information such as forum participation visualization will be provided in the following version of the system.

Group Learning Orchestration Based on Evidence (GLOBE) is a framework for collaborative learning support covering group formation, orchestration, evaluation, and reflection phases, which was put forward for group work support in the data-driven context [12]. This work contributes to the overarching GLOBE framework by bridging the previous group work performance and the next group formation. We aim to utilize the peer evaluation data in the learning log for modeling peer evaluation reliability [15] to tune the evaluation accuracy of peer evaluation. In turn, it can inform the students of their evaluation capabilities and ways to potentially improve them. The evaluation data collected in the system can also be used as inputs to the group formation algorithms [4], and possibly support predictive modeling. With abundant performance data in the future, we can make attempt to explore key factors that make successful group work and generate models to predict the performance of current group work based on previous data of students.

References

1. https://www.mext.go.jp/a_menu/shotou/new-cs/__icsFiles/afieldfile/2017/09/28/1396716_1.pdf
2. Andrade, H.G.: Teaching with rubrics: the good, the bad, and the ugly. Coll. Teach. **53**(1), 27–31 (2005)
3. Bukowski, W.M., Castellanos, M., Persram, R.J.: The current status of peer assessment techniques and sociometric methods. New Dir. Child Adolesc. Dev. **2017**(157), 75–82 (2017)
4. Changhao, L., Botički, I., Ogata, H.: Supporting teachers in group work formation and analytics for in-class group activities. In: ICCE 2019 - 27th International Conference on Computers in Education, Proceedings (2019)
5. Cheng, W., Warren, M.: Having second thoughts: student perceptions before and after a peer assessment exercise. Stud. High. Educ. **22**(2), 233–239 (1997)
6. Cleynen, O., Santa-Maria, G., Magdowski, M., Thévenin, D.: Peer-graded individualised student homework in a single-instructor undergraduate engineering course. Res. Learn. Technol. **28** (2020)

7. Crosbie, R.: Learning the soft skills of leadership. Ind. Commer. Train. **37**(1), 45–51 (2005)
8. Flanagan, B., Ogata, H.: Learning analytics platform in higher education in Japan. Knowl. Manage. E-Learn. Int. J. **10**(4), 469–484 (2018)
9. Gueldenzoph, L.E., May, G.L.: Collaborative peer evaluation: best practices for group member assessments. Bus. Commun. Q. **65**(1), 9–20 (2002)
10. Halavais, A.: Computer-supported collaborative learning. Int. Encycl. Commun. Theory Philos., 1–5 (2016)
11. van Leeuwen, A.: Learning analytics to support teachers during synchronous CSCL: Balancing between overview and overload. J. Learn. Anal. **2**(2), 138–162 (2015)
12. Liang, C., Majumdar, R., Ogata, H.: Learning log-based automatic group formation: system design and classroom implementation study. Res. Pract. Technol. Enhanc. Learn. **16**(1), 1–22 (2021)
13. Mentzer, N., Laux, D., Zissimopoulos, A., Richards, K.A.R.: Peer evaluation of team member effectiveness as a formative educational intervention. J. Technol. Educ. **28**(2), 53–82 (2017)
14. Ollesch, L., Heimbuch, S., Bodemer, D.: Towards an integrated framework of group awareness support for collaborative learning in social media. In: Proceedings of the 27th International Conference on Computers in Education, pp. 121–130 (2019)
15. Piech, C., Huang, J., Chen, Z., Do, C., Ng, A., Koller, D.: Tuned models of peer assessment in MOOCs. arXiv preprint arXiv:1307.2579 (2013)
16. Pond, K., Ul-Haq, R.: Learning to assess students using peer review. Stud. Educ. Eval. **24**, 331–348 (1997)
17. Strauß, S., Rummel, N.: Promoting regulation of equal participation in online collaboration by combining a group awareness tool and adaptive prompts. But does it even matter? Int. J. Comput. Support. Collab. Learn., 1–38 (2021)
18. Strijbos, J.W.: Assessment of (computer-supported) collaborative learning. IEEE Trans. Learn. Technol. (2011)
19. Ismail, N.A., et al.: Peer evaluation system in team work skills assessment. In: Fook, C.Y., Sidhu, G.K., Narasuman, S., Fong, L.L., Abdul Rahman, S.B. (eds.) 7th International Conference on University Learning and Teaching (InCULT 2014) Proceedings, pp. 603–616. Springer, Singapore (2016). https://doi.org/10.1007/978-981-287-664-5_47

Multi-party Video Conferencing System with Gaze Cues Representation for Turn-Taking

Rikuto Iitsuka(✉), Ikkaku Kawaguchi, Buntarou Shizuki, and Shin Takahashi

University of Tsukuba, Tsukuba, Japan
iitsuka@iplab.cs.tsukuba.ac.jp,
{kawaguchi,shizuki,shin}@cs.tsukuba.ac.jp

Abstract. In a multi-party video conference, it is more difficult to achieve smooth turn-taking than in face-to-face communication. This is probably because gaze cues are not shared. In this paper, we propose a system for facilitating turn-taking through the sharing of gaze cues in multi-party video conferences. We implemented video conferencing systems that use arrows and modification of the video window size to share gaze cues the same as in face-to-face communication. We also conducted an experiment to investigate the effect of the system on turn-taking. The results suggested that our system could facilitate turn-taking and communication.

Keywords: Multi-party video conference · Remote communication · Turn-taking · Gaze interaction · Participation status

1 Introduction

In recent years, video conferencing systems such as Zoom[1] and Microsoft Teams[2] have been increasing. However, compared with face-to-face communication, it is difficult to achieve smooth turn-taking in a multi-party video conference, and speech contention and silence often occur. In comparison, in face-to-face communication, there is little speech contention and silence, and smooth turn-taking is achieved. The reason for this is that the participants in face-to-face communication know each other's participation status such as who the speaker is. Gaze cues (information on whom each participant is looking at) play an important role in understanding the participation status. However, in a multi-party video conference, gaze cues are not shared. Therefore, participants are unable to know each other's participation status, and that causes speech contention and silence in turn-taking.

---

[1] https://zoom.us/.

[2] https://www.microsoft.com/ja-jp/microsoft-365/microsoft-teams/free/.

© Springer Nature Switzerland AG 2021
D. Hernández-Leo et al. (Eds.): CollabTech 2021, LNCS 12856, pp. 101–108, 2021.
https://doi.org/10.1007/978-3-030-85071-5_8

To solve this problem, much research has been conducted to promote communication through the sharing of gaze cues in video conferences [5,10]. However, in these studies mainly real space or 3D CG space have been used to represent the relative positions and gaze directions of the participants, and little research has been conducted on video conferences with multi-party participants using 2D video windows such as Zoom and Microsoft Teams.

Therefore, in this paper, we propose a multi-party video conferencing system (Fig. 1) that detects the gaze cues of each participant with a the display-based eye tracking program and visualizes them by using arrows or by modifying of the video window size.

The system aims to promote the understanding of participation status and is expected to reduce speech contention and silence during turn-taking in multi-party video conferencing.

Fig. 1. Proposed multi-party video conferencing systems with two gaze cues representations. Shown are gaze cues represented by arrows (left) and by a change video window size (right). Left and right figures are representations of same gaze cues. Participant in upper left is gazing at participant in upper right, and participants in upper right and below are gazing at participant in upper left.

2   Related Work

Nonverbal information plays an important role in face-to-face communication [9]. Kendon [4] showed that turn-taking is achieved when the speaker gazes at the addressee during a break in speech, and the addressee accepts the gaze and returns it to the speaker (mutual gaze). In addition, the gaze cues of the speaker before the end of an utterance indicate the intention to pass the floor and encourage listeners to be aware of their own participation status. Goffman [3] stated that *the participation status* that each participant has depends on the degree of participation in communication. Participation status include the *speaker* who is currently speaking, the *addressee* who should get the floor next, and the *side participant* who participates in the communication but does not become the addressee. The roles of participants in communication are determined by the gaze cues of the speaker. In addition, the listener's gaze cues influence the speaker's choice of the next speaker [11]. Therefore, participants understand their participation status on the basis of each other's gaze cues [1].

There are many works in which nonverbal information has been used to support turn-taking in video conferencing. Tamaki et al. [8] proposed a method that supports smooth turn-taking in video conferencing by detecting pre-motions before a person speaks and highlighting the participant who is most likely to speak next. A pre-motion is an action that a person performs before speaking, and it expresses the desire to speak. However, Tamaki et al. did not use gaze cues as the pre-motion. Vertegaal et al. [10] proposed a multi-party video conferencing system that transmits eye contact to participants. In this system, the video windows of each participant are arranged in 3D CG space on a the display, and the system turns the video windows to present gaze cues.

Okada et al. [6] conducted a video conference with three people by projecting an actual-size image of the other people on a curved screen and matching their gaze to it. Thus, much research has been conducted to promote communication by sharing gaze cues in video conferences. In these studies mainly real space or 3D CG space have been used to represent the relative positions and gaze directions of the participants. However, existing video conferencing systems such as Zoom and Microsoft Teams display video windows in 2D.

In this paper, we propose a multi-party video conferencing system in which the video windows of each participant are arranged in 2D. In addition, we propose a method for promoting the understanding of the participation status and for facilitating turn-taking in a multi-party video conference by transmitting gaze cues.

3 Proposed System

We implemented a multi-party video conferencing system with gaze cues representation as a Web application.

To implement the system, we used SkyWay [2], a WebRTC platform. SkyWay was also used to send and receive detected gaze directions. A JavaScript library, WebGazer.js [7], was used to detect gaze directions. WebGazer.js detects the point on the display at where the user is looking during a video conference with the built-in camera of a laptop. The detected gaze cues information is sent to each participant using SkyWay and expressed in accordance with each gaze cues representation.

In this research, the video conferencing system is for three participants. The system arranges each of their video window. The system was designed to make one's own window small and the windows of the other participants large. The reason for this was that the results of a preliminary experiment showed that the participants behaved differently from face-to-face communication (e.g., they gazed at their own video window) when the windows were arranged evenly.

Our implemented system represent participants' gaze cues and then shares gaze cues with other participants. We propose two gaze representation methods, which are described in Sect. 3.1.

3.1   Gaze Cues Representation Methods

We proposed two representation methods for visualizing gaze cues. The first represents gaze cues using arrows. The second represents gaze cues by changing the size of the video window.

Method for Representing Gaze Cues with Arrows. Gaze cues of each participant are represented by an arrow (Fig. 1, left). An arrow is displayed on the video screen when the participant is gazing at another participant. However, the arrow that shows who they themselves are gazing at is not displayed on their own screen. Since information on who is looking at whom is shared directly, gaze cues from the speaker can be clearly recognized.

Method for Representing Gaze Cues by Changing Size of Video Window. The video window that many participants are gazing at is enlarged, and the video windows of participants without gaze cues are reduced in size (Fig. 1, right).

In this representation, the participant with the most gaze cues is displayed the largest, making it clear to the listener who to gaze at. There are three window sizes (when no one is gazing, one person is gazing, and two people are gazing), and it does not count when a participant gazes at their own video window. In other words, gaze cues are indirectly shared as the size of the video window. Also, the size of the video window indicates the participation status.

4   Experiment

Using the proposed system, we conducted an experiment to find out whether a video conference using it actually facilitated turn-taking. In this section, we describe the experimental design, results, and discussions.

4.1   Experimental Design

Three participants held a discussion to generate as many ideas as possible by using the video conferencing system. A total of 9 participants (8 men and 1 woman, mean age of 21.7 years) participated. They were split into 3 groups of 3 participants. The following three conditions were set.

- **Control Condition**: video conferencing system with no gaze cues
- **Arrow Condition**: video conferencing system with gaze cues representation method using arrows
- **Window Condition**: video conferencing system with gaze cues representation method using the size of the video window.

The experiment was conducted in a within-subject design. We used a Latin square method for counterbalancing and determined the order of conditions for each group. Each conference lasted for 7 min for each session. At the end of each session, participants completed a questionnaire using a 7-point Likert scale to canvass their subjective evaluation of whether the turn-taking and the conference were facilitated. Table 1 shows the items of the questionnaire.

Table 1. Questionnaire for investigating subjective evaluation of whether turn-taking and conference were facilitated.

	Items
A–1	I think the participants listened to my speech
A–2	I think the participants found I listened to their speech well
A–3	During a break in my speech, I found the next speaker
A–4	During a break in another participant's speech, I found the next speaker
A–5	During a break in another participant's speech, I could speak
A–6	I found who is the speaker is well

We recorded audio and video of the conferences, and we conducted a conversation analysis after the experiment. The ratio of failed turn-takings and the number of utterances of each participant were counted as items to evaluate whether the turn-taking and conference were facilitated. The ratio of the failed of the turn-takings was obtained by dividing the sum of the number of speech contentions and silences by the number of turn-takings.

4.2   Results

Conversation Analysis. First, we conducted a Shapiro-Wilk test and checked the normality (p $>$.05). We also conducted a Bartlett test and checked the homogeneity of variances (p $>$.05).

Second, we conducted a one-way ANOVA on the ratio of failed turn-takings among the three conditions (Fig. 2, left), and there was a marginally significant effect of the condition ($p <$.10). We conducted a multiple comparison test with Bonferroni correction, and we found that the window condition was marginally significantly different compared with the control condition ($p <$.10).

Finally, we conducted a one-way ANOVA on the number of utterances of each participant among the conditions (Fig. 2, right), and there was a significant effect($p = 0.0296 <$.05) of the condition. Under a corrected significance level, a multiple comparison test showed that the window condition was significantly different compared with the control condition ($p = 0.0442 <$.05). We also found the arrow condition was marginally significantly different than the control condition ($p <$.10).

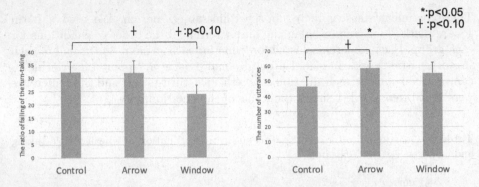

Fig. 2. Results of conversation analysis. Ratio of failed turn-takings (left) and the number of utterances of each participant among three conditions (right) are shown.

Questionnaire for Investigating Subjective Evaluation of the Conference.

The results of the questionnaire are shown in Fig. 3. These items were used to subjectively evaluate whether the system was able to promote participants' understanding of their own participation status in the conference.

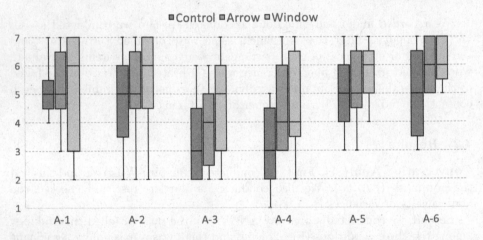

Fig. 3. The results of the questionnaire. These items were used to subjectively evaluate whether the system was able to promote the understanding of their own participation status in the conference. The results for A1 through A6 are shown.

The result of a Friedman's test showed that there was no effect of the condition for all items. However, when the median values were compared, the window condition was rated higher than the control condition for all items. In the arrow condition, the median values of some items were the same as those in the control condition. While turn-taking was promoted, there was no effect of the condition for all items in the subjective evaluation. This could have been caused by a lack in the number of participants.

5 Discussion

In the arrow condition, turn-taking could not be promoted. We also found that participants often looked outside the display. The reason for this could be that the understanding of the participation status was not promoted. Therefore, it might be necessary to further promote this understanding of the participation status in the arrow condition; for example, it might be necessary to consider a design in which one's own gaze cue is displayed on one's video screen, or a design in which one's gaze direction is guided toward the display.

There was a possibility that the window condition promoted the understanding of the participation status. In addition, the number of failed turn-takings decreased, and the number of utterances increased, suggesting that the sharing of gaze cues promotes turn-taking and facilitates conferences in multi-party video conferences. The results of the window condition were also more significant than those of the arrow condition, suggesting that using this method to show the participation status may be effective.

In this experiment, 9 participants were split into 3 groups of 3 participants. However, there were some analysis results that showed no significant differences due to the a lack of data. Therefore, it is necessary to conduct an experiment with more groups as an additional survey to increase the number of pieces of data.

6 Conclusion

The purpose of this study was to reduce speech contention and silences and to facilitate turn-taking in a multi-party video conference. Therefore, we proposed a multi-party video conferencing systems that promotes the understanding of participant status through the sharing of gaze cues.

On the basis of the results of a preliminary experiment, we implemented a video conferencing system promoting gaze cues to be equivalent to those of face-to-face communication and sharing gaze cues. To share gaze cues, we implemented a gaze cues representation method using arrows and one using the size of the video window.

We conducted an experiment to find out whether the proposed system could promote the understanding of participation status and whether it facilitates turn-taking. As a result of the experiment, it was found that our system could facilitate turn-taking and the communication. We also discussed a subjective evaluation of each condition based on the results of a questionnaire, and our findings that will lead to improving the system in the future.

In the future, we plan to improve the gaze cues representation methods based on the findings and conduct experiments with a sufficient number of participants to verify the effectiveness of the proposed system in more detail.

References

1. Bono, M., Suzuki, N., Katagiri, Y.: An analysis of participation structure in conversation based on interaction corpus of ubiquitous sensor data. In: INTERACT, vol. 3, pp. 713–716 (2003)
2. Corporation, N.C.: Skyway. https://webrtc.ecl.ntt.com/
3. Goffman, E.: Replies and responses. Lang. Soc. 5(3), 257–313 (1976). http://www.jstor.org/stable/4166887
4. Kendon, A.: Some functions of gaze-direction in social interaction. Acta Psychol. 26, 22–63 (1967). https://doi.org/10.1016/0001-6918(67)90005-4, https://ci.nii.ac.jp/naid/30008655637/
5. Mukawa, N., Oka, T., Arai, K., Yuasa, M.: What is connected by mutual gaze? User's behavior in video-mediated communication. In: CHI 2005 Extended Abstracts on Human Factors in Computing Systems, CHI EA 2005, pp. 1677–1680. Association for Computing Machinery, New York (2005). https://doi.org/10.1145/1056808.1056995
6. Okada, K.I., Maeda, F., Ichikawaa, Y., Matsushita, Y.: Multiparty videoconferencing at virtual social distance: MAJIC design, pp. 385–393. Association for Computing Machinery, New York (1994). https://doi.org/10.1145/192844.193054
7. Papoutsaki, A., Sangkloy, P., Laskey, J., Daskalova, N., Huang, J., Hays, J.: WebGazer: scalable webcam eye tracking using user interactions. In: Proceedings of the 25th International Joint Conference on Artificial Intelligence (IJCAI), pp. 3839–3845. AAAI (2016)
8. Tamaki, H., Higashino, S., Kobayashi, M., Ihara, M.: Reducing speech contention in web conferences. In: 2011 IEEE/IPSJ International Symposium on Applications and the Internet, pp. 75–81 (2011). https://doi.org/10.1109/SAINT.2011.20
9. Vargas, M.F.: Louder Than Words: An Introduction to Nonverbal Communication. Iowa State University Press (1986). https://ci.nii.ac.jp/ncid/BA0036671X
10. Vertegaal, R.: The gaze groupware system: mediating joint attention in multiparty communication and collaboration. In: Proceedings of the SIGCHI Conference on Human Factors in Computing Systems, CHI 1999, pp. 294–301. Association for Computing Machinery, New York (1999). https://doi.org/10.1145/302979.303065
11. Vertegaal, R., Slagter, R., van der Veer, G., Nijholt, A.: Eye gaze patterns in conversations: there is more to conversational agents than meets the eyes. In: Proceedings of the SIGCHI Conference on Human Factors in Computing Systems, CHI 2001, pp. 301–308. Association for Computing Machinery, New York (2001). https://doi.org/10.1145/365024.365119

Supporting the Initiation of Remote Conversation by Presenting Gaze-Based Awareness Information

Aoto Tanokashira[✉], Ikkaku Kawaguchi, Buntaro Shizuki, and Shin Takahashi

University of Tsukuba, Tsukuba, Japan
tanokashira@iplab.cs.tsukuba.ac.jp,
{kawaguchi,shizuki,shin}@cs.tsukuba.ac.jp

Abstract. Conversations among remote people cannot be easily initiated. A lack of non-verbal information in video calls contributes to the difficulty in initiating conversations. Conversely in face-to-face situations, conversations are initiated by exchanging gaze information, particularly mutual gaze. However, the mutual gaze cannot be easily established between remote locations. In this study, we proposed a voice call system with robots to initiate conversations between remote people by exchanging gaze information. The evaluation results showed that the proposed system was effective in reducing the psychological burden of initiating conversations between remote people.

Keywords: Remote communication · Awareness · Gaze interaction · Informal communication · Communication robot

1 Introduction

Initiating conversations, particularly informal communication, between remote people is difficult. Informal communication occurs incidentally, without a fixed schedule or agenda [2]. To initiate informal communication between people in remote locations, it is necessary to reduce the burden of initiating conversations and make it easier to talk to remote people. Initiating conversations will become easy by understanding whether the remote person is available for conversations. Previous research [4, 7] has realized this assumption by providing awareness information about the remote person's availability for conversations. By contrast, in a face-to-face situation, people use non-verbal information to present the detailed state (e.g., to what extent is the other person focused on a task) of each other, so that they can initiate conversations without disturbing the other person's task. In particular, the exchange of gaze information plays an important role in initiating conversations. When people initiate conversations, they exchange gaze. Mutual gaze is a trigger for initiating conversations. In this study, based on the sociological knowledge about initiating conversations, we reproduced the exchange of gaze that leads to the initiation of conversations between remote

© Springer Nature Switzerland AG 2021
D. Hernández-Leo et al. (Eds.): CollabTech 2021, LNCS 12856, pp. 109–116, 2021.
https://doi.org/10.1007/978-3-030-85071-5_9

people (Fig. 1). We designed a voice call system for remote workers to initiate one-on-one conversations. This system is composed of robots that can exchange gaze between remote locations. When the mutual gaze is established, a voice call starts. We conducted an experiment to clarify the effectiveness of the proposed system.

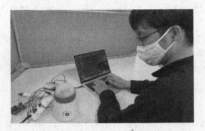

Fig. 1. Actual system setup. Users exchange gaze through the proposed system. When a mutual gaze is established, a voice call starts.

2   Related Work and Our Approach

To initiate conversations between remote people, whether the remote person is available for conversations need to be determined. Previous research has focused on solving this problem by providing awareness information about the remote person's availability for conversations [4,7]. However, only a few works have presented the detailed state of availability that typically precedes conversations in face-to-face situations.

When people initiate conversations in face-to-face situations, they use non-verbal information to present their detailed state to each other. In particular, gaze information plays an important role in initiating a conversation. According to Salvadori [11], before a person initiates a conversation, the initiator assesses the colleague's progress of work and availability. The initiator may use proximity, movement, or gaze to get the colleague's attention. The use of non-verbal information by the initiator allows the colleague to finish his/her task before acknowledging the initiator's request for attention. The colleague displays the termination of his/her tasks by orienting toward the initiator or looking toward the initiator. Thereafter, they start a conversation. Kendon [5] claimed that gaze is a fundamental feature of face-to-face interactions. The shifts of gaze coordinate the timing of speech production. Kendon [6] also showed that mutual gaze can trigger a conversation. Some previous systems [3,8] for presenting awareness information can present not just the availability of a remote user but also non-verbal information. For example, Roussel et al. [10] proposed an always-connected video media space that continuously presents the remote user with non-verbal information. Although these systems are capable of providing non-verbal information, privacy issues still arise because of the use of a video [9].

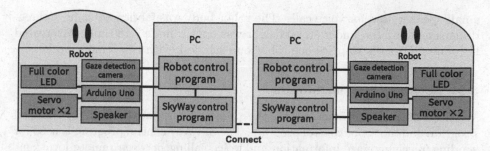

Fig. 2. System configuration.

The exchange of gaze plays an important role in initiating conversations. However, exchanging gaze between remote people without using a video is difficult. In this study, we propose a voice call system with robots to convey gaze information to each other between remote people. The proposed system reproduces the exchange of gaze information that occurs when initiating conversations in face-to-face situations without using a video. The system design is presented as follows: (1) The initiator sends gaze information to the remote person to get the remote person's attention, as in a face-to-face situation. (2) The remote person's response to the initiator's gaze (return gaze or not) is conveyed to the initiator. (3) When a mutual gaze is established, a voice call starts. Based on this system design, the proposed system conveys gaze information to each other through robots placed on each location, which can detect and represent gaze. The initiator can then present the degree to which he/she wants a response based on the length of time he/she sends gaze to the robot.

3   Proposed System

We developed the voice call system with robots that can detect and present gaze and start a voice call. In this section, we describe the hardware, software, and interaction designs of the proposed system. An overview of the proposed system configuration is shown in Fig. 2.

3.1   Hardware Implementation

OMRON's HVC-P2[1] was used for the gaze detection. HVC-P2 can detect the direction of the face and gaze. In the proposed system, we used the face direction detection to detect the user's gaze direction, because the accuracy of the gaze direction sometimes becomes unstable and the reliability is insufficient. HVC-P2 was controlled by a control PC. The detected face direction values were sent to the robot. Two servomotors and full-color LEDs were used to present the gaze. These devices were controlled by Arduino UNO. The robot was equipped with a

---

[1] https://plus-sensing.omron.co.jp/product/hvc-p2.html.

small speaker used for voice calls. The robot body was fabricated using a three-dimensional printer, and its total height was approximately 180 mm. We created two units of robots to place one robot on each desk with two remote workers.

3.2 Software Implementation

We implemented two functions for the proposed system: the SkyWay[2] control program and the robot control program. The SkyWay control program is used for sending/receiving gaze information and voice calling between remote locations. The SkyWay control program sends and receives gaze information and also makes voice calls according to the gaze information.

The robot control program obtains the face direction of a local user from HVC-P2. The robot control program sends the obtained gaze information to the SkyWay control program to convey the gaze information to the remote location. WebSocket is used to communicate with the SkyWay control program. The remote user's gaze information received from the SkyWay control program is sent to the Arduino Uno using serial communication to present the gaze.

3.3 Interaction Design

At the beginning of the interaction, the initiator looks toward the robot. The length of time the initiator sends gaze to the robot conveys the degree to which the initiator wants the remote person's response (Fig. 3-1). For example, if the initiator wants to talk to the remote person who is busy, then the initiator will look toward the robot for a long time. By contrast, if the initiator wants to speak to the remote person when he/she is not busy, then the initiator will look toward the robot for a short time. The remote person returns the gaze if he/she can respond and does not return if he/she cannot. He/she can recognize the degree to which the initiator wants a response from the gaze information presented by the robot (Fig. 3-2). He/she can decide whether to respond or not depending on that degree. If he/she returns the gaze, then a mutual gaze is established through the robot and a voice call starts (Fig. 3-3).

The proposed system changes the color of the eyes according to the gaze information of the users. Basically, the eye color is set to red. When only the initiator is looking toward the remote person, the eye color is yellow. When a mutual gaze is established, the eye color changes to green.

4 Evaluation

4.1 Experimental Design

This experiment aims to evaluate whether the proposed system has more advantages than previous systems in terms of presenting awareness information. Accordingly, we set three hypotheses on the effects of the proposed system.

---

[2] https://webrtc.ecl.ntt.com/.

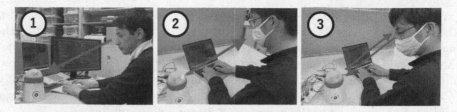

Fig. 3. interaction steps: (1) The initiator sends gaze to the robot. (2) The remote person receives the gaze. (3) The remote person returns the gaze, and a mutual gaze is established.

- **H1.** It reduces the psychological burden of initiating conversations.
- **H2.** It reduces the burden of operating the system to initiate conversations.
- **H3.** It increases the number of attempts to initiate conversations.

To initiate conversations between remote locations, the burden of initiating conversations should to be reduced. Specifically, we focused on the psychological burden and the burden of operating the system. Reproducing the non-verbal interaction in a face-to-face situation before initiating a conversation, it may become easier to talk to the remote person. Thus, the psychological burden of initiating conversations is considered to be reduced (H1). Moreover, by starting voice calls with only gazing, the usability of the system is improved, and the burden of operating the system to initiate conversations is reduced (H2). As a result, the number of attempts to initiate conversations will increase (H3). To test the hypothesis, the following two experimental conditions were set.

- **C1. Gaze Presentation Condition.** This condition was the proposed system in this study. We presented the gaze as the user's awareness information through the robot. When the user wanted to initiate conversations, he/she looked at the robot, and if mutual gazing was established, then a voice call starts.
- **C2. Light Presentation Condition.** In this condition, we used the same system with C1, but did not use gaze detection and presentation function. The users operated the system through the GUI on the PC and made/received a call. The user's availability was presented through light emission. To make it look like a simple LED indicator rather than the actual eyes of the robot, only one of the LEDs in the robot's eye was turned on. Basically, the light was set to red. The light changed to yellow when a voice call was being requested, and if a voice call started, then the light changed to green. This specification was based on the previous system [4,7] providing awareness information about the remote person's availability for conversations.

In this experiment, the participants were asked to do tasks by using a PC according to the a task list(e.g. make a table from multiple data). The participants could interact with the experimenter in another room at any time via the system. The reason for employing an experimenter was to control the contents of the conversation and reduce the effect except of conditions. To evaluate the impression of initiating conversations, the participants needed to talk to the experimenter. Thus, we set several tasks that triggered questions in the task list. To evaluate the impressions of being talked to, the experimenter talked to the participants four times in each trial. The participants sat in front of the PC for the task, and the robot was placed on the left side of the PC (45° from the front of the user). The experiment was conducted in a between-subject design. A total of 20 participants (14 males and 6 females, mean age 22.1 = years, and college students) participated in the experiment, 10 for each condition.

In this study, three assessment items were set to test the hypotheses. To test H1, we conducted the evaluation of impressions related to the psychological burden. We used a questionnaire for evaluating the emotional benefits and costs of communication systems proposed by Yarosh et al. [12]. We used one benefit scale (Presence-In-Absence) and two cost scales (Feeling Obligated and Unmet Expectations) from the questionnaire. We set these scales because we thought that improving the benefit scale (Presence-In-Absence) and decreasing the cost scales (Feeling Obligated and Unmet Expectations) would lead to a reduction in the psychological burden. To test H2, we conducted the evaluation of system usability. We used the System Usability Scale (SUS) [1], which evaluates the usability of a system. To test H3, we analysed the number of attempts to initiate a conversation. We used video recordings of the work for analysis.

4.2   Results and Discussion

In this section, we present and discuss the evaluation results. The first two participants in this experiment were not used in the analysis because of the instability of the system.

Impressions Related to the Psychological Burden. Based on the questionnaire results, Welch's t-test was conducted on the participants' mean scores on each scale. Figure 4 shows a graph of the mean scores for each experimental condition for each scale.

For the Presence-In-Absence scale, a significant difference was found between the conditions ($t(15.63) = 2.44$, $p = .027$). The experiment results showed that presenting gaze significantly improved the effectiveness of conveying the presence of the remote user to the local user. For the Feeling Obligated scale, a significant difference was found between the conditions ($t(11.83) = 2.50$, $p = .028$). The results showed that presenting gaze significantly increased the sense of obligation to communicate. By contrast, the scores were in the positive range (< 4), implying that a negative impression was not given on the sense of obligation in both conditions. For the Unmet Expectations scale, no significant difference was found between the conditions ($t(14.08) = 1.19$, $p = .25$).

System Usability. Based on the questionnaire results, Welch's t-test was conducted on the participants' scores. The mean SUS scores for each condition are shown in Fig. 5. The test results showed no significant difference between the conditions ($t(14.71) = .70$, $p = .49$). Conversely, the mean SUS score (gaze: 81.67, light: 78.06) was high in both conditions [1].

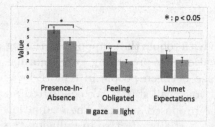
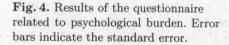

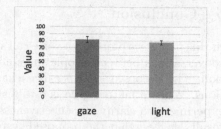

Fig. 4. Results of the questionnaire related to psychological burden. Error bars indicate the standard error.

Fig. 5. Result of SUS. Error bars indicate the standard error.

Number of Attempts to Initiate a Conversation. A Welch's t-test was conducted using the data from the video recording analysis for H3. In the light presentation condition, the mean number of attempts was 2.67 (SE = 0.44). In the gaze presentation condition, the mean number of attempts was 2.78 (SE = 0.55). The test results showed no significant difference between the conditions ($t(15.31) = .16$, $p = .88$).

Discussion. In this study, we set three hypotheses (H1 - H3). For H1, the presence of the remote person could be felt, and it became easy to talk to them. Moreover, the sense of obligation to communicate increased, but not to the extent that a negative impression was produced. These results suggest that the system was partially effective in reducing the psychological burden of initiating conversations, so H1 was partially supported. For H2, although it was not supported, the burden of operating the system to initiate conversations was considered to be small because the system usability was high. For H3, the number of attempts to initiate a conversation did not improve, so H3 was not supported.

The evaluation results suggest that the proposed system was partially effective in reducing the psychological burden of initiating conversations. However, it was not effective in facilitating the initiation of conversations, probably because of the experimental environment. In this experiment, all participants performed a preset task list. Conversations were limited to only the minimum necessary questions in the task, and the number of conversations might depend on the task in the experiment. In addition, an experimenter controlled the contents of the conversation. In a real environment, contents and the number of conversations are not controlled. Hence, in the future, we will conduct experiments in a real environment. Moreover, in this study, whether the results are due to the gaze detection or the gaze presentation is unclear. Thus, we will evaluate the effects of gaze detection and gaze expression separately. The proposed system may result in wrong interpretations among users because the system can only provide limited awareness information through the gaze channel. We will incorporate other non-verbal information into our system.

5   Conclusion

In this paper, we proposed a voice call system with robots that supports initiating conversations between people in remote locations by presenting gaze information. The proposed system can exchange gaze between people in remote locations. When a mutual gaze is established, a voice call starts. We conducted an experiment to clarify the effectiveness of the proposed system. The evaluation results suggest that the proposed system was partially effective in reducing the psychological burden of initiating conversations. Based on the results, it can be said that the burden of operating the system to initiate a conversation is small. However, no significant difference was found between the conditions about the number of attempts to initiate a conversation, which can be attributed to the experimental environment. Thus, int the future, we will conduct experiments in a real environment.

References

1. Brooke, J.: SUS: a quick and dirty' usability. In: Usability Evaluation in Industry, p. 189 (1996)
2. Daft, R., Lengel, R.: Information richness. a new approach to managerial behavior and organization design. In: Research in Organizational Behavior (1983)
3. Dou, M., Shi, Y., Frahm, J.M., Fuchs, H., Mauchly, B., Marathe, M.: Room-sized informal telepresence system. In: 2012 IEEE Virtual Reality Workshops (VRW), pp. 15–18 (2012). https://doi.org/10.1109/VR.2012.6180869
4. Greenberg, S.: Peepholes: low cost awareness of one's community. Presented at the (1996)
5. Kendon, A.: Some functions of gaze-direction in social interaction. Acta Psychologica **26**, 22–63 (1967)
6. Kendon, A.: Conducting interaction: patterns of behavior in focused encounters, vol. 7. CUP Archive (1990)
7. Kuzuoka, H., Greenberg, S.: Mediating awareness and communication through digital but physical surrogates (1999). https://doi.org/10.1145/632716.632725
8. Kuzuoka, H., Kodama, Y., Xu, J., Myodo, E., Harada, E., Osawa, H.: Telepresence robot's salutations to trigger informal conversation with teleworkers. Presented at the (2018)
9. Neustaedter, C., Greenberg, S., Boyle, M.: Balancing privacy and awareness for telecommuters using blur filtration (2003)
10. Roussel, N., Evans, H., Hansen, H.: MirrorSpace: using proximity as an interface to video-mediated communication. In: Ferscha, A., Mattern, F. (eds.) Pervasive 2004. LNCS, vol. 3001, pp. 345–350. Springer, Heidelberg (2004). https://doi.org/10.1007/978-3-540-24646-6_25
11. Salvadori, F.A.: Open office interaction: initiating talk at work (doctoral dissertation). In King's College London (2016)
12. Yarosh, S., Markopoulos, P., Abowd, G.: Towards a questionnaire for measuring affective benefits and costs of communication technologies, pp. 84–96 (2014). https://doi.org/10.1145/2531602.2531634

Author Index

Printed in the United States
by Baker & Taylor Publisher Services